WORDS IN EVERYDAY LIFE

By the same author

AN INTRODUCTION TO OLD ENGLISH
ENGLISH SOUND-CHANGES
THE HARLEY LYRICS *(editor)*
LAYAMON'S *BRUT* *(co-editor with R. F. Leslie)*
A HISTORY OF THE ENGLISH LANGUAGE
ENGLISH DIALECTS
THE MODERN UNIVERSITY
THE LANGUAGE OF DICKENS
VARIETIES OF ENGLISH
THE LANGUAGE OF SHAKESPEARE
BOOKS AND BOOK-COLLECTING

WORDS IN EVERYDAY LIFE

G. L. BROOK

Emeritus Professor of English Language and Medieval English Literature, University of Manchester

First edition 1981
Reprinted 1983

Published by
THE MACMILLAN PRESS LTD
London and Basingstoke
Companies and representatives throughout the world

ISBN 978-0-333-35276-2 **ISBN 978-1-349-06817-3 (eBook)**
DOI 10.1007/978-1-349-06817-3

To John and Joan Levitt

Contents

List of Abbreviations

AN	Anglo-Norman
AV	The Authorised Version of the Bible
COD	*The Concise Oxford Dictionary*
CUP	Cambridge University Press
DNB	*The Dictionary of National Biography*
Fr	French
ME	Middle English
MnE	Modern English
OE	Old English
OED	*The Oxford English Dictionary*
OFr	Old French
ON	Old Norse
ONFr	Old North French
OUP	Oxford University Press
SPE	The Society for Pure English

In Old English words the letters '*þ*' and '*ð*' represent the sound of *th* in *thin* or that of *th* in *then*.

CHAPTER ONE

Words and Phrases

Words have an interest in themselves quite apart from the interest that we may take in the subjects with which they deal. They illustrate the history of the people who use them, but their chief interest is that they enable us to understand how human beings behave and think. By casually turning over the pages of a dictionary we can acquire a surprising amount of miscellaneous knowledge expressed with admirable conciseness. Paul Jennings, who has an eye for such things, discovered in *Chambers's Twentieth Century Dictionary* an entry which should arouse the interest of any well-constituted browser: '**Taghairm**, . . . In the Scottish Highlands, divination; esp. inspiration sought by lying in a bullock's hide behind a waterfall. (Gael.)'. Single words can not only convey pieces of recondite information like this; they can tell us a lot about the thoughts and way of life of our ancestors. *Window* is from ON *vindauga*, a compound of the Scandinavian cognates of *wind* and *eye*. It was the hole in the wall of a house which admitted the light and allowed those inside to look out; in the days before glass was used it also admitted the wind. The poetry of the second element is balanced by the realism of the first. An *eavesdropper* was someone who stood under the eaves of a house in order to hear what was going on inside.

It is a pity that the past beliefs about which words give us information have sometimes in the course of time been shown to be mistaken or inadequate, but that does not destroy the value of words for the historian. *Oxygen* is from French *oxygène*, 'acidifying principle', from a Greek derivative of *oxus* 'sharp, acid', because at first it was thought that oxygen was the essential principle in the formation of acids. *Amethyst* is the name of a precious stone derived from Greek roots meaning 'not intoxicated', because it was thought that it prevented intoxication. Inaccurate ideas about geography are preserved in some nouns derived from proper names: the *guinea-pig* comes not from Guinea but from South America, and the *turkey* is another American bird in spite of its name. The word illustrates the complications that can attach to the study of etymology. It was originally applied to the guinea-fowl because that bird was brought from New Guinea by the Portuguese through Turkish dominions and later applied to the American bird.

Words become even more interesting when they are combined into sentences, but we can understand the sentences better if we know something about the history of the words of which they are composed. There are many different degrees of knowing the meaning of a word. A superficial reader is content if he knows one of its meanings, but most words have a wide range of different senses, and the relation between them repays study. Most of us are content to gain only an approximate idea of the meanings of the words that we encounter while reading, but enjoyment is increased if we read more slowly and discover the exact shade of meaning of at least some of the words. Such care, of course, demands a similar care on the part of the writer, and when we are turning over the pages of a book to find out if it is worth reading, one of the best indications – better even than Alice's test of whether it has any pictures or conversations in it – is the discovery of a word, usually an unexpected one, used in exactly the right way to express a wealth of meaning. I have just had that experience in looking at the first page of a detective story,[1] where there is a reference to 'all those bold, outspoken, competent, middle-aged women whose kind is peculiar to the higher levels of the English *bourgeoisie*, . . . implacably gardening'. I decided that this was a book that I should enjoy.

Opinions differ about the value of a knowledge of etymology. A form of pedantry afflicts some beginners in the study. They find that a word once had a certain meaning and write angry letters to the newspapers complaining of the illiteracy of those who use the word in a different sense. They would save time and paper if they realised that the meanings of a word can and nearly always do change. In reaction against this pedantry we find people saying, as though it were an axiom, that etymology has nothing to do with the meaning of any word, that what matters is the meaning which a speaker or a writer attaches to a word at the time when he uses it. This approach would be reasonable if we could be sure that the speaker knew no more about etymology than his hearers, but there is a good chance that both he and they do know something about the etymology of the words he uses and this knowledge will influence the meaning that he attaches to the words. Both extremes are wrong: we must not assume that because a word once had a particular meaning it will keep that meaning and no other for all time, but on the other hand we cannot afford to ignore etymology completely. It is one of the factors influencing the present-day meaning of words which has to be interpreted in the light of our knowledge of the word's history and of the way in which other words behave.

Greek philosophers often debated whether words and their meanings came 'by nature' or 'by convention'. The Stoics held the former view and attached a lot of importance to the 'true' or original meanings of words. This approach to language is preserved in the word 'etymology', since Greek *etumos* meant 'true'. This view is no longer accepted by serious students of language, though traces of it persist in much general discussion, where arguments are based on the supposed original or essential meaning of a word. If it is a loan-word the true meaning is assumed to be that which is most common in the language from which it is borrowed; if it is a native word many people will assume that the true meaning is the first one given in whatever dictionary they happen to consult. But words are conventional symbols and any word bears the meanings which the speakers of a language have at any given time tacitly agreed to assign to it.

Words are of two kinds: those which have a meaning in themselves and those whose function is to express the relationship of other words to one another. Henry Sweet called the first group 'full words' and the second 'form-words', and these terms are still used. Most nouns and adjectives belong to the first group; most prepositions and conjunctions belong to the second. Form-words are comparatively few in number, but they are of frequent occurrence and they have a wide range of meanings; their study can be regarded as a branch of syntax as much as of semantics. There are dangers in the study of words in isolation, since we all know that a group of words can have an effect greater than that of the sum of its parts, but there are advantages in beginning the study of words by looking at them in isolation before going on to see the effect that they achieve in sentences.

From time to time people fall in love with particular words regardless of their context or, for that matter, their meaning. H. G. Wells's Mr Polly repeated newly discovered polysyllabic words with relish, often getting them wrong. Antony Quinton wrote: 'There are words one falls in love with. I have had affairs with rebarbative and insidious and eleemosynary at various times.'[2] When Rupert Brooke was at school he had an exercise book in which he noted new words as he came across them. To some of these he added the meaning in brackets, as with *frippery* (a shop where old clothes were sold), but others are listed without meanings, since the word was enough: *slidder*, *sluther*, *ombrifuge*, *extravasate*, *arachnoid*, *windlestraws*.[3]

To estimate the size of the vocabulary of any language at a given time is difficult, and the difficulty is greater when we are speaking of the past. The number of words in existence is always far larger than the number that any normal person would understand, and the number that he would understand is usually larger than the vocabulary that he would himself use. There are many derivative words whose meaning may be guessed if the root-word and a few common prefixes, suffixes and inflexional endings are known, even if neither speaker nor hearer has heard the word before. When we are speaking of the past, any estimate must be based on the material that happens to have survived, and no one can say what proportion that bears to the whole body of language spoken and written at the time. The number of recorded Anglo-Saxon words is rather less than fifty thousand; today the number of recorded words is of the order of a million, though most of these are technical terms that are not in general use.

Our vocabulary is constantly being extended. A few, a very few, words, like *gas* and *chortle*, are created deliberately and spontaneously. Some words have come into existence by the imitation of sounds that occur in nature. Words created in this way are often said to be onomatopoeic, but 'echoic' is a better term, because it is shorter and its meaning is clear at once. Words produced by vocal imitation of natural sounds include ***bump, chatter, giggle, hiss, jabber, purr, quack, smash*** and ***thud***. Even echoic words quickly become conventionalised. Do German cocks say kikeriki while in England they say cockadoodledoo? Echoic words can be borrowed into other languages, carrying their conventional components with them; such words are ***bomb, cuckoo*** and ***murmur***. In considering whether a word is echoic, we are concerned with the earliest form of the word. There is nothing particularly echoic about ***laugh***, but it is possible to see an echoic element in its etymon OE ***hliehhan***, in which the ***h***'s were pronounced.

Many words that have been described as echoic owe their origin rather to sound-symbolism. A certain group of sounds may become associated with a particular idea as a result of the accident that it is so associated in a number of words frequently used. Words beginning with *bl-* tend to be violently disparaging; the disparagement spreads from such words as ***bloody, blasted*** and ***blamed*** to ***blessed*** and ***blooming***, which had originally no such associations. Words with [i] often seem to denote things that are small and light, as in ***bit, little, chink, pigmy, slit***, though there will always be exceptions, like ***big***. The group ***fl-*** suggests speed or hurry, as in ***flash, flee, flurry*** and ***fly; -ump*** suggest clumsy and awkward movement, as in ***bump, dump, lump*** and ***thump; gr-*** suggests discontent, as in ***groan, grouse, growl, grumble*** and ***grunt***; and ***st-*** suggests stability, as in ***stable, stand, steadfast*** and ***still***. There is no natural connection between the sounds and the ideas, but the meaning of a word can be influenced by such accidental associations. A probable example of the creation of a new word by this process is ***blizzard***, coined in the United States in the nineteenth century. *OED* suggests that the word is probably 'more or less onomatopoeic' and that it may have been based on such words as ***blow, blast, blister*** and ***bluster***. Many of the names of commercial products that have passed into our everyday language owe something to associations of this kind, though the exact connection may not have been clear to the man who coined the word. *Nylon* may owe something to *cotton* and *rayon*, though one of the most familiar of such words, *kodak*, probably owes its popularity, and perhaps its existence, to its use of clear-cut plosive consonants that are easy to pronounce.

The largest contribution to the extension of our vocabulary has been made by the borrowing of words from other languages. The adoption of a new word is not a sudden process. If the word fails to appeal to more than one user, it remains a mere nonce-usage, to be recorded by lexicographers but never really forming a part of the language. If it satisfies a need, it passes at first through a stage of incomplete acceptance, which may be indicated in the written language by the use of quotation marks or italics and in the spoken language by an apologetic pause during which the speaker wonders whether the word can be used without further explanation. The use of quotation marks round a new word is a matter of personal preference, usually indicating distaste, and it may be indulged in by individuals long after the word has been generally accepted.

The variety of sources of the English vocabulary sometimes leads to confusion. In Latin words *in-* is usually a negative prefix; in native words it has other meanings. Hence *inflammable* is sometimes misunderstood to mean 'not easy to burn', and to avoid confusion it is sometimes replaced by *flammable*.

We do not use the full resources of our rich vocabulary in everyday speech. Barons, viscounts, earls and dukes are all lords, and revolvers, rifles, muskets and cannon are all guns. Words that are applicable to either sex tend to remain in the dictionaries rather than in everyday speech. Siblings are extremely common, but not so the word to denote them. There are as many spouses as husbands and wives put together, but they would be so described only facetiously or in a legal document.

Words may be borrowed not only from foreign languages but from less familiar varieties of the same language, such as regional dialects, slang, archaisms and technical terms. Proper names have provided a large number of words, and many have been created from both native and foreign elements by using the resources of word formation. A small but interesting group of words is that made up of calques, formed by translating the elements of a compound loan-word to produce a word made up of native elements but with its meaning derived from the foreign word, as in *masterpiece*, borrowed in the seventeenth century from Dutch *meesterstuk* or German *meisterstück*, a piece of work by which a workman qualified as a craftsman.

Regional dialects have contributed to the English vocabulary words such as *beck*, *bracken*, *eerie*, *glen*, *heather* and *weird*, which are all from Scottish or northern dialects. Other dialects have made smaller contributions.[4] Lovers of dialects often produce lists of words, such as *fash* 'to bother', *thole* 'to endure' and *nesh* 'soft', which they think might with advantage be introduced into standard English.

In their quest for a wider vocabulary many writers have tried to revive obsolescent words, sometimes with success. Such attempts were particularly common at the time of the Romantic revival and often gave a new meaning or status to the words that were revived. For example, *bard*, as a name for a Celtic strolling minstrel, was a term of contempt before it was revived by Scott, who gave it a new glamour.

Many everyday words have no known etymology, though they have been in the language for many centuries. It is true of words, as it is of place-names, that it is the short ones that cause the most difficulty. No convincing suggestions have been made about the ultimate etymology of such words as *girl*, *boy*, *lad*, *lass*, *big*, *bad*, *dog* or *curse*, although they all occurred before the time of Chaucer. Many monosyllabic words have passed from popular speech into the standard language, including *bleak*, *chop*, *fad*, *fog*, *fun*, *pet*, *skid*, *sniff* and *snore*. Some of these words, such as *cake* and *snob*, have achieved international currency, but little is known of their early history.

Contrasted with these monosyllables, there are polysyllabic coinages some of which no doubt had their origin in jokes, such as *absquatulate* 'to depart', which *COD* suggests may have been based upon *abscond*, *squattle* 'decamp' and *perambulate*. Other examples are *cantankerous*, *harum-scarum*, *higgledy-piggledy* and *pernickety*.

There is a lot of luck in the acceptance of new words. Some of them die almost as soon as they are born; others are mentioned in a book or on a radio programme which happens to arouse popular interest and from this accidental mention they are soon on everybody's lips. Two examples in recent times are *Parkinson's Law*, that work expands to fill the time available, from the book of that name by T. Northcote Parkinson (John Murray, 1958) and the terms *U* and *non-U*, from an article by A. S. C. Ross, first published in a scholarly journal and reprinted in Nancy Mitford's *Noblesse Oblige* (Hamish Hamilton, 1956).

Some new words are the names of new products, such as *nylon*, *antibiotic* and *penicillin*, or of new ways of tackling social problems, such as *ombudsman*. Some are new names for very old things, such as *black market*. A new word may introduce a slight variation in meaning on an existing word, which is then liable to pass out of use. It is a subject for research in both language and social history to decide how far the *macaroni* of the eighteenth century was the same kind of person as the *bounder* or the *teddy boy* of the twentieth, or how the *wangler* of the First World War became the *spiv* of the second.

It is in slang and informal language that we are most likely to find new words. Marghanita Laski has recorded her experience:

> When I'm reading books for the *Oxford English Dictionary*, looking for early examples of words and phrases, I know that when my writer gets solemn I'm going to find nothing, because when he gets solemn his language gets formal, which is to say, old-fashioned, totally lacking any of the novelties or colloquialisms of his time.[5]

Vocabulary can be extended without the creation of any new words by the use of one part of speech for another. This process, known as functional shift, has been particularly common in the Modern English period because of the frequent weakening and loss of inflexional endings in Middle English. As a result of these changes large numbers of verbs became identical in form with their related nouns. For example, OE *lufu* was clearly a noun and OE *lufian* a verb, but by the end of the Middle English period they had both become *love*. Most parts of speech can be affected by functional shift but the most common interchange is between nouns and verbs. We find adverbs being treated as nouns and qualified by adjectives in *somewhere* and *anyhow*, and it is no doubt a feeling that functional shift is wrong that causes many Americans to say *some place* rather than *somewhere* and many people in both England and America to prefer *anyway* to *anyhow*. The use of abstract nouns as verbs meets with opposition, and many people do not like to hear verbs like *to contact* or the librarian's *to accession*, but the use of a noun as a verb may introduce a useful shade of meaning: *to audition* means more than *to hear*. The use of verbs as nouns is generally colloquial: an advertiser may assure his readers that a bargain is *a good buy* or that an indispensable object is *a must*. Functional shift is sometimes disguised by the disappearance of the word in its original function. Thus the verb *to leer* is from the Old English noun *hlēor* 'cheek'. Nouns are often used as adjectives. It is not always easy to distinguish between a noun used as an adjective and the same noun used in apposition with another noun. A test is provided by the greater freedom with which adjectives can be used as compared with nouns. They can be used predicatively, they can show degrees of comparison and they can be qualified by the adverb *very*. If we apply such tests we can see that *large* is undoubtedly an adjective, since expressions like *the building is large*, *larger* and *very large* seem perfectly natural, but we achieve unnatural results if we treat *model* in *model aeroplane* in the same way. There are intermediate stages which allow words to pass some, but not all, of these tests. We can say *this furniture is utility* but we should not normally say that it is *very utility*.

In Anglo-Saxon times a number of words were given special Christian applications which changed their meanings so drastically that they became virtually new words. *Fiend* (OE *fēond*) meant 'enemy' but came to mean 'devil'; *worship* (OE *weorþscipu*) at first meant 'honour' but came to refer especially to the honour paid to God; *doom* (OE *dōm* 'judgement') came to refer to the Last Judgement and is often used in the compound *Doomsday*. *Bless* underwent a transference rather than a narrowing of meaning: OE *bletsian* is a derivative of *blōd* 'blood' and originally referred to consecration by blood sacrifice.

In Middle English the additions to our vocabulary consisted chiefly of loan-words from other languages, but in native words Middle English was prolific in verbs indicating movement formed with the suffixes *-er* or *-le*. Thus we have *chatter*, *scatter*, *shudder*, *totter*; *hobble*, *mumble*, *nibble*, *sparkle*.

In Elizabethan times the English vocabulary continued to be extended by the introduction of loan-words, but other methods were used, such as the re-introduction of obsolete English words, the creation of new compounds and the application of new meanings to old words. These methods are all illustrated in the language of Shakespeare and they are all in use at the present day. It is a matter of some surprise that to denote the new inventions of the last century or so, such as the gramophone and television, we have chosen words from Latin or Greek, languages that were spoken when those inventions were unknown. One reason is that the classical languages lend themselves to word formation in the coining of new compounds; another is that new words formed in this way can be easily understood by the speakers of other European languages and so enjoy an international currency.

Some well-known words are of surprisingly recent introduction. *Adenoids*, *aspirant*, *environment*, *radium*, *reliable*, *scientist* and *talented* were first recorded in the nineteenth century. More recent still are *anorak*, *boutique*, *dirndl*, *espresso*, *marijuana*, *ombudsman*, *sauna*, *scampi*, *schizophrenia*, *voyeur* and *zombie*. Some widely used scientific terms were superseded soon after their introduction. Few people now speak of a phonograph, and those who speak of a gramophone are likely to be told 'You mean a record-player'. It has often been pointed out that words reflect social history both in the introduction of new words and in the revival of old ones. The increase in the number of crimes of violence in recent years accounts for the increased frequency of the word *mugging*, and the scarcity of houses has encouraged the practice of *gazumping*, raising the price of a house after accepting an offer. The word is a recent coinage of unknown etymology.

Some words, like *tandem*, preserve a joke. The Latin adverb *tandem* 'at length' referred to time. It was applied in jest to two horses in harness one behind the other and then, with the invention of the bicycle, it was transferred as an appropriate name for a bicycle made for two. *Sesquipedalian*, an adjective meaning 'many-syllabled', preserves a joke made in another language. Horace spoke of *sesquipedalia verba*, 'words one and a half feet long' (*Ars Poetica*, 97), and the word was borrowed into English at the time of the Restoration.

For the most part the English vocabulary has been built up by thousands of anonymous contributors. Diligent searches in the *Oxford English Dictionary* make it possible to compile lists of words first recorded in the works of this or that famous author, but they do not answer the question of where he got them from. He may have coined them, but the further back we go the more necessary is it to remember the mass of unrecorded material that underlies our recorded literature. There are a few words, however, whose inventors are known. We have learnt to distrust anecdotal etymologies, but we must accept the etymology of *serendipity*, 'the art of making happy discoveries by accident'. It was coined by Horace Walpole in a letter to Horace Mann on 28 January 1754, because this faculty was possessed by the heroes of a fairy tale *The Three Princes of Serendip*, an old name for Ceylon. We have to distinguish between the first recorded use of a word, which may be due to the accident of preservation, and deliberate invention claimed as such, but there are some words which can with reasonable probability be assigned to particular authors. Dryden coined *witticism* on the analogy of *criticism* in 1677. Sterne coined *lackadaisical* to describe people who were always saying lackaday. *Publicist* was coined by Burke in 1792 and *pantisocracy* by Coleridge and Southey. Coleridge coined many words that have never been much used and a few that have become established, like *relativity* and *transitional*. Jeremy Bentham coined *international* and Napier coined *logarithm*. William Whewell coined *scientist* in 1840 and T. H. Huxley coined *agnostic* in 1869. *Gas* was coined by J. B. van Helmont, a Belgian scientist who died in 1644.

Those whose attempts to introduce new words meet with little success can derive consolation from the reflection that many words now familiar were greeted with derision when they were first introduced. Ben Jonson derided his rival Marston's fondness for new words and quoted with scorn such words as *clumsy*, *puffy*, *reciprocal* and *strenuous*.[6]

Novelty is not the only reason why words are avoided. A common reason is the opposite one that they have been over-used by second-rate writers trying to create an impression of magnificence. Such words are *commence*, *inaugurate* and *portion*. Other words may be avoided because they are obvious euphemisms, like *casket* for 'coffin', *deceased* and *senior citizen*. We like to avoid words that have unpleasant associations but we do not like to be seen too obviously to be doing so. Over-emotional terms of abuse may be seized upon with derision by those at whom they are aimed, and their use in parody causes their inventors to lose their enthusiasm for them. Thus we find many men describing themselves proudly as male chauvinist pigs.

There has been a constant search for new ways of expressing emphasis, and *awfully* and *tremendously* have become mere synonyms for 'very'. Hence these emphatic words tend to have a short life as intensives, as when Coriolanus is said to be 'vengeance proud' (II. 2.6). Literary terms like *epic*, *dramatic* and *tragedy* have been over-used by journalists in search of emphasis, and more careful writers therefore use them only when they must.

We cannot always find a reason why words denoting everyday ideas have passed out of use. There often seems to be no obvious reason for their disappearance. Logan Pearsall Smith[7] uses the apt metaphor 'blight' to denote the fate that inexplicably befalls some words whose position in the language seemed secure. They first of all disappear from colloquial speech while continuing to be used in writing. The next stage is that they are driven from the vocabulary of prose to that of verse and finally they disappear into the limbo of archaisms and affectations. Such words are *bide* 'wait', *blithe* 'glad', *dight* 'clothed', *fain* 'glad', *fell* 'fierce', *mar* 'spoil', *rathe* 'early', *rue* 'regret', *teen* 'grief' and *woe* 'sorrow'. Some of these archaisms, such as *slay* and *sooth*, remain chiefly in facetious use; some, such as *delve* and *dwell*, remain as metaphors but are not often used literally. The theory put forward by Robert Bridges that words disappear when they become homophones accounts for only a small number of disappearances, because identity of form is not enough to cause a word to disappear; there must also be similarity of function. An example is provided by the two verbs *let*. OE *lǣtan* 'to allow' and OE *lettan* 'to prevent' have fallen together as *let* and the two verbs resemble each other in function, so that it is not always obvious from the context which word is intended. It is therefore natural that one of the words should pass out of use except in specialised contexts, and this has been the fate of *let* 'to prevent', except when we speak of a let at tennis or use the phrase 'without let or hindrance'. One common cause of death is excessive use; schoolchildren are advised to avoid words like *get* or *nice* because such words are used too often and many people find it easier to obey a ban than to practise moderation. Another cause of disappearance is the use of a once-dignified word in trivial contexts, which makes people self-conscious about using it. This process is easily observable in the choice of forenames, some of which are liable to arouse derision if given to children today. If a list of such names is examined, it will be found to include the names of many noble families and of heroes famous in history or legend.

The death of words is always slow and rarely complete. All that we can hope to do in discussing obsolescent words is to say that they have passed out of general use, but they linger on in a neglected old age, occasionally used by old-fashioned speakers or by those who feel a distaste for their fashionable replacements. Some words, instead of dying, survive in a specialised sense. Thus, from the thirteenth century the verb *cut*, of unknown origin, began to replace OE *snīþan*, which disappeared, and OE *ceorfan*, which survives as *carve* in the specialised senses of cutting up meat and the craft of decoration. The Old English verb meaning 'to throw' was *weorpan* and this became specialised as *warp*. A piece of wood which dries out of shape is said to warp and we use the word figuratively when we speak of a man having a warped mind. In the general sense of 'throw' OE *weorpan* was replaced by *cast* (ON *kasta*), which in its turn acquired many specialised senses; in its general sense it was replaced by *throw*, from OE *þrāwan* 'to twist'. In slang *throw* is often replaced by verbs felt to be more vigorous, such as *chuck*. A few words have passed out of use because by phonetic change they have become too short to be easily recognisible. This may be the reason why OE *ēa* 'river' has been replaced by the loan-word *river*.

One reason why the metaphor 'death' is not a good one to denote the obsolescence of words is that the process is reversible. Words that have become unfashionable may be restored to use for no very obvious reason. *Kid* 'child' underwent the fate of most slang words in becoming unfashionable, but it has recently become more popular again, especially in the plural with undertones of affection. *Kid brother* is often used with the sense 'younger brother'.

Many words have passed out of general use while surviving in particular social groups or families or in regional dialects. Such a word is *nesh* (OE *hnesce* 'soft'), which is used in dialects in a pejorative sense. A mother, urging a child to go out and play instead of huddling over the fire, will tell it not to be so nesh. The north-country *thoil* 'tolerate', used especially in relation to the spending of money, preserves OE *þolian* 'to endure'. The Scottish phrase 'to dree one's weird' contains two words which were well established in Old English: *drēogan* 'to endure' and *wyrd* 'fate'. The first of these has passed out of use in standard English; the second has survived as an adjective with a meaning that is a result of a misunderstanding of Shakespeare's reference to the Weird Sisters in *Macbeth*. The Scottish dialects have preserved several of the words that have virtually disappeared from standard English, such as *greet* 'to weep' (OE *grēotan*), *fey* 'fated to die' (OE *fǣge*) and *gang* 'to go' (OE *gangan* 'to walk').

The word is a convenient unit, but it is often possible to recognise groups of words that have been used together so often that the group can be considered as a unit in itself. Such groups are sometimes called idioms and sometimes clichés, and it is not always easy to distinguish between them. An idiom is a group of words peculiar to one language which by usage is given a meaning which cannot be deduced immediately from the separate words of which it is composed. A cliché is a phrase that has been weakened by excessive use. Whether we call a phrase an idiom or a cliché generally depends on whether we like it or not, but such phrases form an important element in a language. Imperfect mastery of idiom is one of the signs by which foreigners can be recognised. The most convenient test of an idiom is: can it be translated word for word into a foreign language without producing nonsense? By this test phrases like 'How do you do?', 'far and away' and 'you are right' can be seen to be idiomatic. Ludicrous results can be achieved if a speaker with an imperfect command of a foreign language translates into it the elements of an idiom from this own language, as when two Englishmen, crossing the Alps, stayed the night at a monastery where only Latin was to be spoken. One of the Englishmen soon broke the rule and his friend thought it necessary to utter a warning: 'Nunc tunc'.

Idioms are essentially a part of the language of everyday life. Logan Pearsall Smith has summed up the place of idioms in English:

> Since our idioms, whether of English or foreign growth, are . . . so largely of popular origin, we should hardly expect to find abstract thought embodied in them, or scientific observation, or aesthetic appreciation, or psychological analysis of any subtle kind; – and these indeed are almost completely lacking. The subject-matter of idiom is human life in its simpler aspects; prudent and foolish conduct, success and failure, and above all human relations – the vivid attitudes and feelings of people intensely interested in each other and their mutual dealings – approval, but far more largely disapproval, friendly but more often hostile feelings, fallings out and makings up, rivalries and over-reachings, reprobation, chastisement, and abuse.[8]

Almost every human activity has given rise to phrases which have passed into everyday use, often with some change of meaning. From mining we have 'to peter out', from railways 'to go off the rails'. From a joke in *Punch* in 1895 we have 'the curate's egg', parts of which were excellent. From the navy we have 'to clear the decks', 'to find one's bearings', 'to know the ropes', 'to make headway', 'to steer clear of someone', 'to take the wind out of his sails' and 'in the offing'. From the army we have 'to call a halt', 'a false alarm', 'the rank and file', 'to spike his guns' and 'to stand one's ground'. From farming we have 'to be in clover', 'to put one's hand to the plough', 'to break fresh ground' and 'to plough a lonely furrow', and from commerce we have 'taking stock', 'making the best of a bad bargain' and 'cutting our losses'.

Idioms often show a vigour of imagery of the kind that we expect from slang, and some idioms are slang. We use idioms so often that we do not as a rule pause to think of the images that they conjure up, but a lively imagination has gone to the coining of such expressions as 'a bull in a china shop', 'making a silk purse out of a sow's ear' and 'teaching one's grandmother to suck eggs'.

Idioms arise naturally from the activities of everyday life, like falling between two stools. It is natural that images from cooking should be widely used: 'to butter somebody up', 'to be in hot water', 'to keep the pot boiling', 'to have other fish to fry', 'to make a hash of something', 'to put the lid on it', 'out of the frying-pan into the fire', 'it's the pot calling the kettle black' and 'to cry over spilt milk'. Many of these idioms are proverbs, short pithy sayings, based on the affairs of everyday life. If taken literally they may be either patently true, like 'half a loaf is better than no bread' or 'you can't make an omelette without breaking eggs', or patently false, like 'a watched pot never boils', but they contain the sort of homely wisdom that is passed down from mother to daughter and from father to son. Some of them are so well known that there is no need to quote them in full, as when we say that there are too many cooks, or a proverbial phrase may be used, as when we describe a fuss about nothing as a storm in a teacup or an easy but well-paid task as money for jam.

Many idioms arose when handicrafts played a more active part in everyday life than they do today. When every village had its blacksmith it was natural that people should see the advantages of striking while the iron was hot or the disadvantages of having too many irons in the fire. If disagreements arose it was natural that they should be hammered out or ironed out. It was obviously dangerous to play with edged tools, and for some activities it was best not to put too fine a point on it. All these idioms have survived in everyday use although the activities that gave rise to them are no longer everyday.

One group of phrases which are clearly popular in origin

consists of comparisons with animals. In course of time certain animals have acquired good or bad reputations, and the widespread fondness for stereotypes has attributed a single quality to each animal. These qualities form the basis of such phrases as 'blind as a bat', 'sly as a fox', 'stubborn as a mule', 'busy as a bee', 'hungry as a wolf' and 'to work like a beaver'. The comparison may be compressed into a metaphor, and most people would understand the meaning of such words as *pig*, *bear*, *fox*, *serpent*, *drone*, *cat*, *bitch* or *vixen* when applied to a human being. A more complicated stereotype was that of the schoolboy who wrote: 'Pigs are rightly so called for they are such swine'.

Readiness to use clichés is generally a result of indifference to the finer shades in the use of language, and the same indifference can lead to the inappropriate use of words, which may cause a phrase denoting violent action to be used on a trivial occasion. The cliché 'heads will roll' generally means that somebody will receive a mild reprimand, and very few of the people who say that they will tear someone limb from limb have either the strength or the intention to carry out the threat. Clichés from the nursery generally have a mildly humorous intention, as when someone says ruefully that he has egg on his face or advises a friend to keep his nose clean.

It is not always easy to distinguish between a cliché and a proverb. Since *cliché* is a term of abuse, we may perhaps accept the distinction that a man who uses a cliché is not as a rule conscious that the phrase is well worn and conventional, whereas the man who quotes a proverb is conscious that he is quoting a piece of anonymous conventional wisdom pithily expressed.

There are many phrases consisting of pairs of near-synonyms linked by 'and': 'rough and tumble', 'high and mighty', 'heart and soul', 'law and order', 'dust and ashes', 'down and out', 'by fits and starts', 'by leaps and bounds', 'odds and ends', 'free and easy'. These phrases are sometimes repetitions of the same word, by which the speaker seeks to gain emphasis: 'again and again', 'by and by', 'round and round', 'share and share alike', 'over and over again'. The link between the two words may be one of contrast, as in 'give and take', 'ups and downs', 'through thick and thin'. Sometimes alliteration seems to have led to the choice of one of the words of a pair, as in 'chop and change', 'rough and ready', 'safe and sound', 'at sixes and sevens', and sometimes it is rhyme, as in 'fair and square', 'high and dry', 'wear and tear'. In such pairs we often find that only one word carries the burden of meaning; the other word may be archaic or rare or used with a forced and unusual meaning. Sometimes both words are rare outside the idiomatic phrase, as in 'spick and span', 'scot and lot'. How does one moil and what is a lurch? We know the words today only in the phrases 'toil and moil' and 'leave in the lurch'. *Kith* is rarely used except when linked by alliteration with *kin*. *Kith* means 'acquaintances' and therefore forms a natural pair with *kin* 'relatives'.

Some comparisons, with the same help from alliteration, have become so well established in the language that from being idioms they have become clichés: 'as bold as brass', 'as cool as a cucumber', 'as fit as a fiddle', 'as good as gold'.

Foreigners find life in England difficult because our interest in sport and games has given to the language a large number of idioms that express disapproval. Shooting a fox, bidding no trumps without top honours and potting the red are things that are not done. To be told that these things are not cricket is simply another idiom that the hapless visitor has to acquire.

Some phrases which, when used legitimately, make a useful distinction tend to be avoided because people are vague about their precise meaning when they are used as technical terms. We all know the everyday meaning of the phrase 'at arm's length' used to denote keeping far enough away from someone to avoid undue familiarity, but the phrase is a technical term used in financial reports of dealings where neither party is controlled by the other. Another phrase is 'above the line', which most of us associate with scoring at bridge. The precise meaning, as defined by Kenneth Hudson,[9] is that an above-the-line cost is one that is to be charged to a particular budget whereas anything below the line is ordinary expenditure. At first this may seem to belong to the language of accountancy, but it is a distinction that often has to be made in everyday life, as when we are deciding whether to go to work by car or bus or how much to pay for making a call on a neighbour's telephone.

CHAPTER TWO

Loan-words

The term 'loan-word' is used to denote a word taken from a foreign language and used as though it were native to the language into which it has been borrowed. A widespread belief crops up from time to time in several languages that the use of loan-words is in some way discreditable. The French have coined the blend-word *franglais* to denote a variety of French that has too many English loan-words, and admirers of German describe it as 'pure' because it uses compound words made up of native elements to express many ideas for which we, in English, use loan-words.

English has an unusually large number of loan-words, and these have added to the number of near-synonyms in the language as well as providing new words to express new ideas. Those who like loan-words describe English as having 'a rich vocabulary', but there is no special virtue in having a lot of words in a language; they make it harder to learn and, in so far as the loan-words add to the number of exact synonyms, they are a nuisance. If they add to the number of near-synonyms, they are an asset, provided that the users of the language are sensitive to the different shades of meaning that attach themselves to such pairs as *hearty* and *cordial* or *motherly* and *maternal*. The problem is one that generally solves itself. If a loan-word earns its keep by expressing a shade of meaning that cannot be expressed by a native word, it will remain in use; if it serves no useful purpose, there is a good chance that it will disappear.

A loan-word may pass through several different languages, each of which may have an effect on its form and meaning. The ultimate history of a word may contain surprises. We are right if we think that *kraal* is borrowed from South Africa, but wrong if we think that it was originally a Boer or Zulu word. It was borrowed into South African English from Portuguese *curral*.

The borrowing of words from different languages has led to the creation of many homophones, pairs of words which are pronounced and spelt alike although they differ in origin and meaning. It is on the basis of such accidental resemblances that puns are made. A golfer's *caddie*, who carries his clubs, gets his name from a Scots dialect development of French *cadet* 'younger son', which has also given us *cad*, whereas *caddy* in *tea-caddy* 'a small box' is from a Malay word denoting a weight of one and one-third pounds.

A study of the dates of introduction of familiar loan-words can be instructive. Many of the financial activities of today had their roots in the seventeenth century, and from that period we have words like *commercial*, *discount*, *insurance* and *investment*.

There are few Celtic loan-words in Old English because the Celts with whom the English invaders came into contact had mostly been Romanised. Possible examples that have survived today are *bannock* 'loaf', *bin*, *brock* 'badger', *dun* 'dark-coloured' and the dialectal *brat* 'apron'. Later loans from Welsh are *coracle*, *cromlech*, *eisteddfod*, *flannel* and *flummery*, originally denoting a kind of porridge. From Scots Gaelic we have *cateran*, *claymore*, *gillie*, *glen*, *loch*, *plaid*, *ptarmigan*, *slogan*, *sporran* and *whisky*. From Irish we have *banshee*, *bog*, *colleen*, *galloglass*, *galore*, *kern*, *shamrock*, *shillelagh*, *Tory* and *usquebaugh*. There are many place-names of Celtic origin, especially river-names like *Avon* and *Ouse*.

The earliest Latin loan-words were borrowed into Common Germanic or West Germanic before the speakers of these languages crossed to Britain, and many of them have survived until today. They include *mile*, *wall*, *wine* and various derivatives of Latin *caupo* 'innkeeper', such as *chapman*, *cheap* and *Cheapside*. Other trade terms introduced at this time are *inch*, *mint* and *pound*. Some of these early loans, such as *cheese*, *cook*, *kitchen* and *mill*, are closely concerned with the affairs of everyday life. The Roman occupation of Britain had provided a few words taken into English from the Romanised Britons. *Street* is from Latin *strata via* 'paved road', and Latin *castra* 'camp' provided the second element of many place-names, such as *Winchester* and *Worcester*. The Romans imposed their rule on most of the world that was known to them and, either directly or through French, we have borrowed from them many words connected with government, such as *authority*, *dictator*, *empire*, *officer* and *rule*.

The introduction of Christianity into England brought with it many Latin loan-words, some of them ultimately from Greek, to denote Christian ideas, such as *abbot*, *angel*, *bishop*, *canon*, *deacon*, *monk* and *priest*. From Latin too we have names of plants and animals, like *lily* and *tiger*. Some loan-words were borrowed again later. Latin *elephant-* gave OE *elpend* but the Modern English form was borrowed through Old French.

It is not easy to estimate the extent of Latin influence on Middle English because the large influx of French words included many words, like *attention* and *position*, which might equally well have been borrowed from Latin or French, and words that had been borrowed from Latin were often reshaped to make them resemble French words.

Latin loan-words preserve many different Latin inflexions, as may be seen in such words as *affidavit*, *bonus*, *deficit*, *errata*, *folio*, *innuendo*, *memorandum*, *nostrum*, *quorum*, *recipe*, *referendum* and *veto*. The reason for the diversity of inflexional endings is that some of the Latin words formed a part of phrases from which we have borrowed only a single word. For example, *folio* is from the ablative of Latin *folium* 'leaf', from its use in references specifying a particular leaf. Sometimes the endings have been dropped, as in *verb. sap.* 'a word to the wise (is enough)'. *Recipe* 'take' is an imperative because it is the first word of a doctor's prescription used by metonymy for the whole document. *Nostrum* means 'our own'; it denotes a proprietary remedy not known to other doctors and it is easy to see how it came to mean 'a quack medicine'. *Innuendo* is from the ablative gerund of Latin *nuo* 'to nod' and it refers to the practice of making an oblique hint by nodding in a particular direction, using no words that could be quoted. *Memorandum* is from the neuter singular gerundive of Latin *memorare* 'to remember' and it denotes something that must be remembered. *Bonus* is a comparatively recent borrowing, and that may be the reason why it was borrowed in the masculine instead of the neuter *bonum* 'a good thing'. It was borrowed after Latin had passed out of general use, when people took Latin words from dictionaries, not from sentences.

The revival of learning in the fifteenth and sixteenth centuries led to a great increase in the number of Latin loan-words. Many Latin words and phrases have passed into everyday use from the language of the law, though they are still recognised as legal terms, such as *alias*, *alibi*, *bona fide*, *proviso* and *subpoena*.

Most early loans from Greek have come to us through Latin. *Devil* (OE *dēofol*) was a loan into Common Germanic, as was *church* (Greek *kuriakon*) '(house) of the Lord'. In the later language Greek influence on medicine is to be seen in *dropsy*, *quinsy* and *treacle*. Literary terms of Greek origin include *comedy*, *drama*, *elegy*, *epic*, *epigram*, *lyric*, *ode*, *poetry*, *prologue*, *rhapsody*, *rhythm* and *tragedy* and metrical terms such as *anapaest* and *dactyl*. Rhetorical terms include *apostrophe*, *climax*, *colon*, *comma*, *hyphen*, *idiom*, *paragraph*, *paraphrase* and *rhetoric*. Some of the terms of learned origin have become everyday words, like *harmony*, *history* and *music*. *Ambrosia* and *nectar*, the Greek words for the food and drink of the gods, are today used chiefly in advertising.

The resemblances between Old English and Old Norse were so close that many words were identical in the two languages, and we therefore cannot be certain whether they are loan-words or not. Sometimes the form of the word gives an indication of its origin by showing the result of a sound-change in one of the two languages. The group *sk* remained in Old Norse, whereas in Old English it gave a sound which was spelt *sc* and is today spelt *sh*. Thus *shirt* is the native cognate of the Scandinavian loan-word *skirt*. In native words, but not in Scandinavian, *k* was palatalised before front vowels to the sound that is now spelt *ch*. Consequently such words as *kettle* and *kirk* can be recognised as Scandinavian loan-words.

The best-known fact about Scandinavian loan-words in English is that they are generally familiar, everyday words; words like *anger*, *give*, *hit*, *husband*, *ill*, *take*, *ugly*, *want*, *wrong* and the pronouns *they*, *their* and *them* are not thought of as loan-words. They were borrowed because the relations between the English and the Scandinavians were close and their two cultures similar. We do not find, as we do with French loan-words, that the foreigners were the teachers and the natives the pupils, absorbing new ideas with the words to describe them. One reason why Scandinavian words have been so completely assimilated is that they were borrowed early, and they have undergone changes in form and meaning along with native words. There are some hybrids, such as *awkward* and *greyhound*.

There was a time-lag between Scandinavian settlements and the appearance of their loan-words in texts; there are not many before about 1200. The reason is that Scandinavian influence was strongest in the Danelaw, and not many texts have survived from this part of the country before the thirteenth century. The strength of Scandinavian linguistic influence can best be judged from place-names. The North has large numbers of place-names containing Scandinavian elements like *-by* and *-thwaite*.

The Scandinavians did not impose their own language on the parts of England that they occupied, probably because they came in small numbers at a time and found a settled civilisation similar to their own to which they could attach themselves. The experience contrasted with that of the English invaders of Britain, who had imposed their own language on the conquered country.

The close resemblances between English and the Scandinavian languages led to the development of doublets, one word native and the other Scandinavian. We often find that both words have survived with a divergence of meaning, as in *whole* and *hale*, *no* and *nay*, *shirt* and *skirt*, *from* and *fro*, *-less* and *loose*, and *rear* and *raise*, which are both causatives of *rise*. The meaning of the Scandinavian cognate has sometimes affected that of the native word. OE *drēam* meant 'joy'; MnE *dream* has derived its meaning from the Scandinavian cognate *draumr*. *Dwell* is from OE *dwellan* 'to lead astray' but its modern meaning 'to abide' is from ON *dvelja*. In Old English *loft* meant 'air, sky'; the modern meaning 'attic' is from the cognate ON *lopt*. *Earl* is from OE *eorl* 'warrior', but its use as a title is derived from the Old Norse cognate *jarl*. *Plough* is from OE *plōh* 'measure of land'; the modern sense is from ON *plógr*. OE *blōma* meant 'a mass of molten metal'; the sense of MnE *bloom* has been influenced by ON *blómi* as well, perhaps, as OE *blōstma* 'blossom'. OE *holm* meant 'sea'; the modern meaning 'island' is from Scandinavian. Sometimes one word of the pair has become obsolete, like the native plural *eyren*, used by Caxton, but now replaced by the Scandinavian *eggs*. Sometimes one word of the pair survives in standard English but the other only in dialects, as in *loup* beside *leap* and *garth* beside *yard*.

Sometimes a common native word has been replaced by a Scandinavian word of similar meaning but quite different form and etymology. For example, OE *niman* has been replaced by ON *taka*, OE *steorfan* has been replaced in its wider sense by ON *deyja*, and the native word *welkin* (cf. OE *wolcen* 'cloud') has been replaced by the Scandinavian *sky*. There has been differentiation of meaning in *skin* and *hide*, the former (ON *skinn*) applying to human beings as well as animals, the latter (OE *hȳd*) only to animals. Some words that were rare in Old English have been reinforced by Scandinavian influence. Such words are *dale*, *call* and the preposition *till*.

A few Scandinavian words have been borrowed in post-medieval times, such as *dahlia*, *eider(down)*, *fiord*, *geyser*, *ski*, *troll* and *tungsten*. Scholars interested in Scandinavian literature have introduced such words as *edda*, *Norn*, *saga*, *valkyrie* and *viking*.

Scandinavian words are common in the modern dialects of northern and eastern England. Examples are *addle* 'to earn', *flit* 'to move, especially when moving to a new house', the adjective *gain* 'direct', *lake* 'to play' and *war* (rhyming with *far*) 'worse'. A concise piece of Yorkshire discouragement is 'tha mends war', i.e. 'instead of improving you are getting worse'.

A few French words were in use in England before the Norman Conquest, including some that have survived until the present day, such as *bacon*, *capon*, *castle*, *market*, *proud* and *tower*. Whereas Scandinavian influence was mainly on the language of everyday life, French influence was most marked in the language of the upper classes, though it was so strong that no social class escaped it completely. The two languages French and English remained in use side by side in England for several centuries. Since the French held all the important positions, their influence on the language was out of all proportion to their numbers. This influence was strengthened by the links that they maintained with the Continent, which led to their reinforcement by constant streams of French-speaking newcomers.

In the course of the Middle English period there was a gradual decline in the use of Anglo-Norman. When English came to be used more generally, there was an increase in the use of French loan-words, since the upper classes, who could speak French, were now beginning to use English as their normal language. The greatest influx of French loans was in the period 1250–1400. Up to the end of the twelfth century the influence was chiefly from Anglo-Norman; after that it was from Central French.

One of the motives for the borrowing of French words was to provide synonyms or near-synonyms of native words that poets could use to satisfy the demands of rhyme, alliteration and metre and to express different shades of meaning. Examples of pairs of near-synonyms, one native the other French, are *begin* and *commence*, *child* and *infant*, *help* and *aid*, *hide* and *conceal*, *wedding* and *marriage*. There are pairs where it is hard to see any distinction in meaning, such as *shire* and *county*, *thief* and *robber*, *weapons* and *arms*. The introduction of French loan-words was accompanied by a decline in the Old English fondness for compound words and for derivation by the use of affixes. A native word might be completely replaced by a French synonym or it might survive only in dialects. OE *ēam* 'uncle' survives as *eme* in Scots, and OE *flītan* 'to contend' has survived in dialectal *flyte*.

A great weariness descends on most readers of books on the history of the English language when they are confronted with lists of French loan-words in Middle English classified according to subject. French words are so easily recognisable and their number so large that most readers can compile their own lists or consult those that are readily available.[1] It may seem more profitable to find fields that are not well represented by many French loan-words. Such subjects are seafaring and parts of the body. We may take a single field, that of the law, to illustrate the large number of French loans and the way in which they are treated in English. Legal terms include *adultery*, *arson*, *burglary*, *coroner*, *crime*, *embezzle*, *entail*, *equity*, *estate*, *flotsam*, *jetsam*, *jettison*, *judgement*, *jury*, *justice*, *lease*, *legacy*, *libel*, *perjury*, *rejoinder*, *repeal*, *slander*, and the phrases *hue and cry* and *treasure trove*. French influence causes the adjective to follow the noun in *attorney general*, *court martial*, *malice prepense* and its partial translation *malice aforethought*. The French form of a word was sometimes kept, even when it was contrary to English linguistic habits, as in *lèse majesté*, *puisne* (a doublet of *puny*) and *oyez*, used by the town-crier. Some French legal terms have undergone a change of meaning. Anglo-Norman *asetz*, a variant of OFr *asez* 'enough', was taken to be a plural noun and has given our *assets*. The original meaning of *assize* was 'a sitting down'; *premises* were 'the things aforesaid', a technical term first in logic and then in law; *culprit* is from the Anglo-Norman phrase *culpable: prest d'averrer* '(you are) guilty and (I am) ready to prove it'.

We have borrowed many French words that are so familiar that we never think of them as loan-words, verbs like *aim*, *allow*, *carry*, *cover*, *grant*, *reply* and *wait*, and adjectives like *able*, *brief*, *chief*, *common*, *gentle* and *strange*. The large number of loan-words denoting familiar ideas suggests a warning about the use of loan-words to provide evidence for the study of social history. Some loan-words denote new objects or new ideas, but many of them denote familiar ideas and there is no obvious reason why they should be borrowed.

At the Restoration there was a revival of French influence on the language as the returning exiles brought back French ideas and customs. Many of the words borrowed at this time have kept their French pronunciations, as in *ballet*, *contretemps*, *décor* and *métier*. Serjeantson points out[2] that there are few French loans first recorded between 1600 and 1640 and they are chiefly military or diplomatic words like *brigade*, *dragoon*, *fanfare*, *parole* and *stockade*. In the second half the century there are more loan-words dealing with literature and amusement, such as *burlesque*, *memoirs*, *repartee* and *tableau*. In the eighteenth and nineteenth centuries we find new words dealing with the arts, such as *belles lettres*, *connoisseur*, *critique*, *salon* and *savant*, with fashion, such as *chenille*, *corduroy* and *rouge*, and with food, such as *cuisine*, *liqueur*, *meringue* and *rissole*. French loans of the last two or three centuries contain a smaller proportion of everyday words than the early loans. They are easily recognisable as loan-words.

From the other European languages we have nothing to compare with the flood of words from French, but virtually every language has made some contribution. From German we have *alpenstock*, *carouse*, *festschrift*, *hinterland*, *kindergarten*, *plunder*, *poodle*, *rucksack* and *yodel*. German influence was strong in the science of mineralogy, and we therefore have *bismuth*, *cobalt*, *gneiss*, *quartz*, *shale* and *zinc*. More recent words are *blitz* and *ersatz*. There are several calques, translating into English the elements of German compound words, such as *standpoint* from *Standpunkt*, *homesickness* from *Heimweh*, and Shaw's *superman* from Nietzsche's *Uebermensch*.

Low German and Dutch resemble Old English so closely that some apparent loans may be cognates identical in form with Old English words that happen not to have been recorded. There were shipping and commercial links between the Low Germans and the English because English wool and Flemish weavers were the best. *Pack* and *selvedge* are from the wool trade. Other trade terms are *excise*, *guilder* and *huckster*. Military words were brought back by English mercenaries from the Low Countries in the sixteenth and seventeenth centuries, such as the verb *cashier*, *drill*, *furlough*, *knapsack*, *onslaught* and *tattoo*. Naval terms include *belay*, *boom*, *bowsprit*, *buoy*, *caboose*, *commodore*, *cruise*, *deck*, *dock*, *keel*, *reef*, *skipper*, *sloop*, *smack*, *swab*, *yacht* and *yawl*. Commercial terms include *brandy*, *hawker*, *isinglass*, *smuggle* and *stoker*. Art terms include *easel*, *etching*, *landscape*, *maulstick*, *sketch* and *stipple*. Non-technical terms are *boor*, *booze*, *groove*, *heyday*, *hops*, *loiter*, *poll*, *sloven* and *spool*. *Gin* is from Dutch *genever*, ultimately from Latin *juniperus*. *Forlorn hope* is from Dutch *verloren hoop* 'lost expedition'; Dutch *hoop* is cognate with English *heap*.

Italian influence was strong in the sixteenth century. Roger Ascham (d. 1568) complained of the 'Englishman Italianate', who came back from his travels using too many Italian words. A large number of early Italian loan-words, such as *alarm*, *alert*, *artisan* and *caprice*, have reached us through French. Many Italian loans dealing with art and music have become a part of the common European vocabulary of technical terms.

There was contact between England and Italy from the fourteenth century through trade and banking, an influence of which we have a record today in the name *Lombard Street*, one of the centres of London banking. Fourteenth-century loans include *brigand*, *ducat*, *florin* and *million*. From the fifteenth century Flemish ships called at English ports on their way to and from Venice. In the sixteenth century we find trade terms, such as *bankrupt*, *contraband*, *frigate*, *milliner* and *traffic*, and items of merchandise, such as *artichoke* and *porcelain*. From the end of the sixteenth century commercial influence declined but cultural influence increased. There were some military terms, such as *bandit*, *battalion*, *citadel*, *duel* and *squadron*.

Musical terms reached their peak in the eighteenth century, but they are found in an unbroken stream from the sixteenth. They include *aria*, *cantata*, *concerto*, *madrigal*, *mandolin*, *opera*, *oratorio*, *pianoforte*, *piccolo*, *serenade*, *sonata*, *soprano*, *spinet*, *trombone* and *violoncello*. Many Italian terms belong to the technical vocabulary of music, but some, like *piano*, *prima donna*, *trio* and *violin*, have passed into everyday use. The directions on musical scores are generally given in Italian. They are thought of as Italian words used in a specialised context and have not passed into the everyday language. They include such terms as *andante*, *tremolo* and *ma non troppo*.

Many architectural terms were borrowed in the sixteenth century, such as *cornice*, *cupola*, *pedestal*, *piazza* and *stucco*. New terms were added in the seventeenth century, such as *balcony*, *grotto* and *portico*, and in the eighteenth, *arcade* and *colonnade*. There are many words dealing with painting and sculpture: *baroque*, *cameo*, *cartoon*, *filigree*, *fresco*, *mezzotint*, *miniature*, *picturesque*, *replica*, *studio*, *terra cotta*, *tempera* and *torso*. Italian literary influence is strong in the works of Chaucer but it does not become widespread until the Renaissance; loans are *burlesque*, *canto*, *sonnet* and *stanza*. There are many words for food and drink, such as *broccoli*, *chianti*, *macaroni*, *semolina*, *spaghetti*, *vermicelli*, and for customs and social habits, such as *carnival*, *casino*, *conversazione*, *gala*, *gazette*, *gondola*, *incognito*, *parasol*, *regatta* and *vendetta*.

Borrowings from Spanish on a large scale began in the sixteenth century, when Spain was at the height of her national power. Spanish words of this period borrowed directly or through French include *armada*, *bravado*, *comrade*, *galleon*, *grandee*, *grenade*, *negro*, *peccadillo*, *punctilio*, *renegade* and *tornado*. Later words from Spanish are *brocade*, *capsize*, *cargo*, *cork*, *desperado*, *embargo*, *esplanade*, *guerrilla* and *mosquito*. Spanish activities in America led to the introduction of words from Mexico and the West Indies, such as *barbecue*, *cannibal*, *chocolate*, *cocoa*, *maize*, *mulatto*, *potato*, *tobacco*, *tomato* and *vanilla*. American influence is to be seen in some words of Spanish origin, such as *alligator*, from Spanish *el lagarto* 'the lizard', used to denote an animal which the Spanish found in Florida. Many Spanish words borrowed into American English have passed into British English with American rather than Spanish associations. Examples are *bonanza*, *cafeteria*, *canyon*, *chaparral*, *cinch*, *corral*, *lariat*, *lasso*, *ranch*, *silo* and the slang *vamoose*.

As explorers the Spanish concentrated on the Western hemisphere while the Portuguese colonised Brazil and turned east to Asia and Africa. From their language we borrowed *flamingo* and *molasses* in the sixteenth century. Other loans are *buffalo*, *caste*, *cobra*, *fetish*, *madeira*, *mandarin* and *yam*. *Port*, from the place-name Oporto, was borrowed at the end of the seventeenth century. From India through Portuguese we have *pagoda*. *Padre* is a Portuguese word which acquired its religious sense in the east. *Palaver* was first used to denote a conference with Africans. *Massage* came to use through French in the nineteenth century from Portuguese *amassar* 'to knead'.

Most of our loans from Russian are used to denote Russian products or institutions, such as *balalaika*, *bolshevik*, *czar*, *knout*, *kopek*, *menshevik*, *mujik*, *pogrom*, *rouble*, *samovar* and *soviet*. Such restriction is in contrast with our borrowings from a language like Greek, which has given us many words dealing with more universal ideas. Some Russian loans are words which Russian had first borrowed from the West and modified, such as *intelligentsia* and *commissar*. From other Slavonic languages we have borrowed directly or indirectly *cravat*, *howitzer*, *mazurka* and *robot*. From the non-Indo-European language Hungarian we have borrowed *coach*, *shako*, *tokay* and *vampire*.

From America we have many names of plants, animals and products which have kept their American associations, such as *alpaca*, *caoutchouc*, *cassava*, *cayman*, *condor*, *guava*, *ipecacuanha*, *jaguar*, *llama*, *pampa*, *puma* and *tapir*, all brought to Europe by one or other of the colonising powers from the West Indies or South America. Some words from these sources, such as *cannibal*, *canoe* and *hurricane*, have lost their specifically American associations. From North American Indian languages we have many words that are still thought of as American, such as *hickory*, *hominy*, *moccasin*, *moose*, *opossum*, *pemmican*, *raccoon*, *skunk*, *squaw*, *succotash*, *terrapin*, *toboggan*, *tomahawk*, *wampum*, *wigwam* and the slang *mugwump*, now generally used as a mere term of abuse but derived from an Algonquin word meaning 'great chief'. It owes its unfavourable meaning to its ironical use to denote a man who holds aloof from party politics. Disliked by both parties, a mugwump was said to be a man who sits on the fence with his mug on one side and his wump on the other.

Several words, such as *chowder*, *picayune* and *prairie*, were borrowed from the French in America. From Spanish were borrowed *calaboose*, *Creole*, *quadroon* and *stampede*. From Dutch came *boss*, *cookie*, *snoop* and *waffle*, and from German *delicatessen*, *frankfurter*, *hamburger*, *lager* and *schnitzel*. These words are understood in British English but most of them have kept their American flavour. On the other hand, many Americanisms have been so thoroughly assimilated into British English that most people who use them are unaware of their American origin. Such words are *belittle*, *boarding-house*, *businessman*, *governmental*, *graveyard*, *law-abiding*, *lengthy*, *overcoat* and *telegram*.

Most of the words borrowed from the languages of Asia and Africa denote ideas or products connected with their countries of origin and when used today they have kept those associations. Some of the words have been borrowed into most European languages. The language of this group that has influenced English over the longest period is Arabic. The earliest Arabic loan is *mancus*, used as money of account in Anglo-Saxon times, though there is not much evidence of the use of the coin itself in England. Several Arabic loans denote products of Greek culture which reached Western Europe through the Arabs when direct links between Greece and Western Europe were broken. These include *alchemy*, *alembic*, *carat*, *elixir* and *talisman*. The Crusades led to contacts between the Arabs and the nations of Western Europe that made the borrowing of words possible. Direct loans from Arabic include *albatross*, *alkali*, *attar*, *azimuth*, *emir*, *fakir*, *fellah*, *harem*, *hegira*, *hookah*, *islam*, *koran*, *mohair*, *moslem*, *muezzin*, *mufti* and *sheik*. There are many indirect borrowings, such as *admiral*, *alcohol*, *alcove*, *algebra*, *amber*, *arabesque*, *artichoke*, *assassin*, *azure*, *bedouin*, *caraway*, *carmine*, *cotton*, *crimson*, *gazelle*, *ghoul*, *giraffe*, *magazine*, *mattress*, *minaret*, *mosque*, *mummy*, *naphtha*, *ogive*, *orange*, *saffron*, *senna*, *sirocco*, *sofa*, *sugar*, *sultan*, *tabor*, *talc*, *tariff*, *vizier* and *zenith*.

There are some doublets among Arabic loans. An Arabic word meaning 'drink' has been borrowed directly into English in the forms *sherbert* and *shrub*; borrowed through Spanish and French it has given *syrup*. Arabic *sifr*, borrowed through Spanish and French, has given *cipher*; through Low Latin and Italian it has given *zero*.

The number of direct loans from Hebrew is not large, because most of the ideas of the Old Testament have reached us through Greek or Latin. Words of Hebrew origin include *amen*, *cherub*, *jubilee*, *manna*, *rabbi*, *sabbath*, *seraph* and *shibboleth*. Beside these religious terms we have a number of names of products, plants and animals, such as *camel*, *cassia*, *cider*, *cinnamon*, *ebony*, *elephant*, *hyssop*, *leviathan*, *nitre*, *sapphire* and *shekel*.

Yiddish was originally a Middle Rhine dialect of German, used by Jews; the word is derived from German *jüdisch* 'Jewish'. The language includes many Hebrew loan-words, and such words as *kosher* 'genuine' and *goy* 'Gentile' may be regarded as loans from either Hebrew or Yiddish. Many of the words that we have borrowed from Yiddish are slang, like *nosh* 'snack'. *Oof* 'money' is from Yiddish *ooftisch*, from German *auf dem tische* 'on the table', applied to money used in gambling. A *kibitzer* is a meddlesome person who gives unwanted advice, especially when watching a game of cards from behind the players; it is from Yiddish *kibitser*, a derivative of German *Kiebitz* 'lapwing', which came to mean 'busybody' and has to be distinguished from the common Hebrew loan-word *kibbutz*, the term applied to a co-operative settlement in Israel. Another Yiddish loan based on a German word of different meaning is *schmaltz*, used to denote sugary sentimentalism, especially in music, from German *Schmalz* 'dripping, lard'. There are many phrases in colloquial English which probably show Jewish influence. Leo Rosten includes among them 'get lost', 'you should live so long', 'I need it like a hole in the head', 'OK by me', 'I should have such luck' and 'wear it in good health'.[3]

One of the earliest loans from India is *rajah* 'prince', borrowed in the sixteenth century. The East India Company was founded in 1600, and from that time there has been a steady stream of loan-words, most of which have kept their eastern associations, such as *coolie*, *durbar*, *nabob*, *rupee* and *sepoy*. More general loans are *bangle*, *bungalow*, *cheroot*, *cot*, *dinghy* and *shampoo*. The earliest loans were chiefly names of products, such as *chintz*, *indigo* and *jute*, or of animals, such as *cheetah* and *mongoose*. In the nineteenth century the study of Indian philosophy led to the introduction of Sanskrit religious terms, such as *avatar*, *karma*, *nirvana*, *swastika* and *yoga*. Other nineteenth-century loans are *loot*, *polo*, *puttee*, *pyjamas* and *thug*.

From Persian we have borrowed several words, often by indirect routes. Examples are *azure*, *borax*, *caravan*, *check*, *chess*, *chicanery*, *divan*, *jasmine*, *julep*, *kiosk*, *lemon*, *lilac*, *mogul*, *pasha*, *satrap*, *scarlet*, *scimitar*, *shah*, *shawl*, *spinach*, *taffeta*, *tulip* and *turban*.

The few words that we have borrowed from Turkish nearly all refer to aspects of Turkish life. They include *horde*, *turquoise*, *uhlan* and *coffee*, which is ultimately of Arabic origin.

We have borrowed several words from Malay either directly or through the languages of European explorers and traders. Direct borrowings include *amok*, *caddy*, *gong*, *gutta-percha*, *kapok*, *orang-utan*, *paddy*, *rattan*, *sago* and *sarong*. From Malay through Dutch we have borrowed *cockatoo* and *gingham*. Through French we have *junk* 'ship' and through Spanish *launch* 'boat'. From Tongan we have *taboo* and from Hawaiian the recent loan *ukulele*.

There are not many loans from China or Japan. From Chinese we have *chop-suey*, *ginseng*, *serge* and *tea*, and from Japanese we have *hara-kiri*, *jinrickshaw*, *ju-jitsu*, *kamikaze*, *kimono*, *netsuke*, *samurai*, *satsuma* and *soya*.

In South Africa the Dutch and the English satisfied the need for an extended vocabulary in different ways. The Dutch used the resources of their own language by modifying the meaning of Dutch words to meet African needs or by forming compounds; the English borrowed words freely from both African languages and Dutch. The variety of Dutch used in South Africa is known as Afrikaans, and from it we have borrowed such words as *eland*, *hartebeest*, *spoor*, *springbok*, *trek* and *veldt*. Words borrowed from African languages, including some from more northerly parts of the continent, are *chimpanzee*, *gnu*, *gorilla*, *tsetse*, *voodoo* and *zebra*.

Settlers in Australia borrowed a few words from aboriginal languages, but they made greater use of their own language in finding names for the new animals they encountered, either by using the names of English animals or by forming compounds. Words from aboriginal languages are *boomerang*, *budgerigar*, *corroboree*, *kangaroo*, *koala* and *wombat*. Words made up from European elements to denote Australian birds or animals include *honey-eater*, *lyre-bird* and *laughing jackass*, a bird which got its name because its harsh call resembles the braying of a donkey. A well-established word referring to Australian natural conditions is the *outback* to denote a remote inland district.

The existence of large numbers of loan-words in English has increased the possibilities of convergence and divergence of words in form and meaning. Convergence adds to the difficulty of using the language by making possible deliberate or unconscious puns and leaving a speaker uncertain whether he is concerned with one word or two. It can lead to ambiguity, which may cause one word of a pair to pass out of use. Thus, *ancient* 'old' is from French *ancien*, but Iago was Othello's *ancient*, a corruption of *ensign* from OFr *enseigne*. It is not surprising that the latter word is now archaic. Divergence is especially common in loan-words because variations in date and dialect in the languages from which these words are borrowed produce the differences of form which made divergence possible. Divergence of form is often followed by divergence of meaning, and the result is that we have two different words from a single source. Such pairs are known as doublets. *Minster* and *monastery* are early and late borrowings from Latin and there is a similar relation between *priest* and *presbyter*. *Skirt* is from the Scandinavian cognate of the native English *shirt*. The archaic *wain* is a doublet of *wagon*; the former is from OE *wægn* and the latter is from its Dutch cognate *waghen*.

The largest group of doublets in English consists of French loan-words which were reinforced by borrowings of the Latin words from which they were ultimately derived. The Latin word was sometimes borrowed directly; sometimes it was borrowed through French. *Dainty* and *dignity* are both derived ultimately from Latin *dignitas*. Latin *ratio* has been borrowed three times: it became OFr *resoun*, and this gave us *reason*; later *ration* was borrowed into French and thence into English in the sense of a fixed daily allowance of food; and later still *ratio* was borrowed directly from Latin into English as a mathematical term. Similarly Latin *gentilis* became OFr *gentil*, which was borrowed into English as *gentle*; the word was borrowed again with spellings that represented the contemporary French pronunciations as *genteel* and *jaunty*; a borrowing more closely modelled on the Latin has given *gentile*. *Chamber* is from OFr *chambre* from Latin *camera*; direct borrowing from Latin has given *camera*. *Sire* and *sir* are from French *sire*, and *sirrah* is an angry or scornful pronunciation; the Latin etymon is *senior*, which has been borrowed directly in that form. Other similar pairs are *blame* and *blaspheme*, *debt* and *debit*, *balm* and *balsam*, *frail* and *fragile*, *chance* and *cadence*, *poison* and *potion*, *poor* and *pauper*, *count* and *compute*, *dungeon* and *dominion* and *sure* and *secure*. Sometimes one word of the pair has become obsolete, as in *parfit* beside *perfect* and *peynture* beside *picture*.

The variation between two words may arise entirely in English. *Metal* is a loan-word from French or Latin and *mettle* is a variant spelling. In Elizabethan times the two spellings were interchangeable but today we keep *metal* for the literal meaning and *mettle* for the figurative sense 'the quality of a person's disposition'. The difference between two words of a pair may be one of stress with or without a difference of spelling. When *conjure* has the stress on its first syllable, it means 'to produce apparently magical effects'; when the stress is on the second syllable, the meaning is 'to invoke'. Accent variation has been followed by differences in spelling, pronunciation and meaning in such pairs as *human* and *humane* and *antic* and *antique*.

CHAPTER THREE

Words from Proper Names

Many words are derived from the names of persons or places well-known in history or literature; others are based on forgotten anecdotes or on men whose memory is kept alive only by the words which their names have contributed to the English vocabulary. It is often difficult to say whether a given word is a proper name or not. Eric Partridge's *Name Into Word* (Secker and Warburg, 1949) has an appendix of 165 pages of border-line words which are sometimes regarded as proper names, sometimes as common nouns. The use of an initial capital is an unreliable guide.

Words derived from proper names can be classified according to their parts of speech or, more profitably, according to their source: places, persons, characters in literature and so forth. Nouns are the most numerous, more so than adjectives and verbs put together. Proper names often become nouns with no change except the loss of the initial capital. They can become verbs without change, as in *hector*, or with the addition of an affix, as in *macadamise* and *enslave*. The different categories of words from proper names are innumerable. Inventors give their names to their inventions. Products are named after the part of the world from which they come or from which they were believed to have come. Commercial products pass into general use, taking their names with them, but the names do not always become common nouns. The test is whether the name can be transferred without awkwardness to the product of a rival firm. A *thermos flask* can be used as a general term for any make of vacuum flask and we find a similar development in such words as *biro*, *kodak*, *elastoplast*, *sellotape* and *Scotch tape*.

Some words are derived from the names of persons about whom little or nothing is known. *Derrick* 'hoisting contrivance' originally meant 'hangman' or 'gallows' and is derived from the name of a hangman at Tyburn *c.* 1600. In dialects there are comparisons like 'as throng as Throp's wife' or 'as lazy as Ludlam's dog' in frequent use by speakers who have no idea who Throp or Ludlam were, except for the information that Ludlam's dog leaned up against the wall when it wanted to bark. A forename is often adopted as a common noun, and it may have a wide range of meanings. Workmen become fond of the tools they use and give them affectionate nicknames. We therefore find forenames, especially in their pet forms, applied to tools, like a *spinning jenny*, a burglar's *jemmy* and an Australian bushman's *billy* or kettle. *Jack* is found with many different meanings, as in *jack-knife, jack-in-the-box, jackanapes, black jack* and a *jack* for lifting a car.

Words formed from proper names undergo changes just like words of other origins. They can be curtailed, as in *strad* for *stradivarius*, a violin made by Antonio Stradivari (d. 1737) in Cremona, or *pom* for *Pomeranian* or *peke* for *Pekingese*. They can be disguised by the addition of prefixes or suffixes, as in *antimacassar*, a protection against oil from Macassar in the East Indies, or *macadamise* 'to pave a road surface with small broken stones', from John Loudon Macadam (d. 1836), a Scottish civil engineer, or *mercerise* 'to strengthen cotton fabrics' from John Mercer (d. 1866), who discovered the process in 1850, *pasteurise* from Louis Pasteur (d. 1895), *grangerise* 'to illustrate a book by inserting prints' from James Granger (d. 1776), or *balkanise* 'to divide a region into small states like the countries of the Balkan Peninsula'. Words derived from proper names can be blended with other words, as in *gerrymander* 'to manipulate electoral divisions', which is a blend of *salamander* with *gerry* from Elbridge Gerry (d. 1814), who used this device to make sure that the Republicans remained in power in Massachusetts. By functional shift a noun formed from a proper name may be used as another part of speech, as in the verb *meander* from a river in Phrygia or the adjective *maudlin* from Mary Magdalene. Their meanings may be drastically changed, as in *bedlam*, *vandal*, *slave* and *gypsy*.

Many words have passed into our everyday language from Greek and Roman mythology, many of them as derivatives. *Panic* was originally an adjective meaning 'concerned with the god Pan' and it referred to the fear inspired by the mysterious sounds heard in the open air in the country; the rural god Pan had come to be regarded as the personification of nature. The activities of the devotees of Bacchus, the Greek god of wine, were known as *Bacchanalian*, and the adjective is often linked with *revelry* in a cliché to denote a festive party in which wine plays a large part. Atropos was one of the three Fates who had the task of cutting the thread of human life to the required length; *atropine* thus became a picturesque term for a poisonous alkaloid found in the deadly nightshade. Atlas was a giant who supported the heavens on his shoulders; the use of *atlas* to denote a book of maps is said to be due to Mercator's use as a frontispiece of a picture of Atlas supporting the globe. Tantalos was a mythical king of Phrygia who was condemned to stand in Tartarus surrounded by water and fruit that was just out of his reach. The Latinised form of his name, *tantalus*, was thus an appropriate term for a spirit-stand in which decanters are locked up but visible, and his name has given us the verb *to tantalise*. Another word derived from Greek legend is *Procrustean* 'tending to produce uniformity by violent methods'; Procrustes was a violent robber of Attica who stretched or amputated his victims to make them fit his bed. The Titans, a race of giants, have given us *titanic*. Eros, the Greek god of love, has given us *erotic*, and the goddess Aphrodite has given us *aphrodisiac*. *Hermetic* is derived from Hermes, a versatile god whose responsibilities included occult sciences, especially alchemy; it is used today chiefly in the phrase *hermetic seal*, an airtight closure by fusion used by alchemists. A river of the Greek underworld has contributed to the meaning of *lethal*, from Latin *lethum* 'death' associated with Greek Lethe, the waters of which produced oblivion. Another river of the underworld, the Styx, has given us *Stygian*, chiefly used in the cliché *Stygian gloom*. The Greek goddess of retribution has given us *nemesis*, and *music* is from a Greek adjective denoting the art of the Muses. *Siren* has changed its meaning. The Greek sirens were creatures half woman, half bird, who lured sailors to a rocky island with their singing, but today we more often use the word to denote an instrument giving a loud sound as a warning. In the Second World War we became familiar with the *siren suit*, a one-piece garment for the whole body, easy to put on when one was aroused by an air-raid siren.

From Roman mythology we have *mercury* and the adjective *mercurial* from Latin Mercurius. As the messenger of the gods he had to move quickly, and mercury responds quickly to a slight movement of the hand on which it rests; the adjective is applied to a person who is subject to quick changes of mood. A *flora*, a methodical description of the plants of a particular region, is from Flora, the Roman goddess of flowers.

From Greek literature we have taken the names of philosophers and attached them to selected aspects of their teaching, often misunderstood. *Platonic* is defined by *COD* as 'confined to words or theory, not leading to action, harmless', which seems to be faint praise, but the most common use of the word today is to denote purely spiritual love as contrasted with erotic or sexual desire. An *Epicurean* is a follower of Epicurus, a man of gentle and frugal habits who taught that the highest good is calmness of mind. He would not have supported the belief in the importance of sensual pleasure which is generally associated with his name today. His beliefs are usually contrasted with those of the *Stoics*, followers of Zeno, who taught in the Stoa, or porch, in the market-place at Athens, advocating control of the passions and indifference to pleasure and pain. From the *Iliad* we have *Nestor*, who has become the type of the wise old man, and *stentorian* from Stentor, a herald with a powerful voice, and from the *Odyssey* we have *Mentor*, the experienced adviser of Telemachus. Hector has been badly treated in English. The noun now means 'a bully' and the verb derived from it means 'to browbeat'. Hector was the most valiant of the sons of Priam. In earlier English literature he is regarded as the type of a gallant warrior, but in the seventeenth century gangs of disorderly young men who fancied themselves as 'Hectors' disturbed the streets of London, and the meaning of the word took a turn for the worse. The verb *pander* is from the Trojan Pandarus, but his unsavoury activities as a go-between are from the later treatments of the legend by Chaucer and Shakespeare.

From Roman mythology we have *cereal* from Ceres, the goddess of agriculture. The name of Cupid, the god of love, is clearly related to *cupidity*. *Fate* is from Latin *fatum* 'that which is spoken', hence 'doom (of the gods)'; it came to mean the power by which events are determined. There was similar personification in Fortuna, the goddess of chance as a power in human affairs, and Gratia, one of the three goddess sisters who bestowed beauty and charm. From these we get *fortune* and *grace*.

Greek and Roman history have given us a few words. Some of the characteristics of the Spartans are recorded in our use of *Spartan* to denote simplicity and endurance and of *laconic* to denote speech that is concise and sententious, since Laconia was another name for Sparta. From Roman history we have taken the adjective *Augustan*, which primarily indicated resemblance to the first Roman emperor Augustus Caesar (d. AD 14), but which has come to mean an outstanding period of Latin or any other literature. In England it refers especially to the literature of the late seventeenth and early eighteenth centuries. An English political movement took its name from Quintus Fabius Maximus, who died in 203 BC and earned the name Cunctator by harassing the Carthaginians while avoiding open battle. The Fabian Society, founded in 1883 and supported by Sidney Webb and Bernard Shaw, advocated a gradual approach to socialism in contrast with the revolutionary beliefs of Marx.

From the Bible we have *abigail* 'a lady's maid'. In 1 Samuel 25.24 Abigail speaks of herself as David's handmaid, and Abigail is the name of a 'waiting gentlewoman' in Beaumont and Fletcher's *The Scornful Lady* (1616). The character reinforced the meaning of the word, which has always had a slightly literary flavour. The loss of the initial capital has disguised the origin of *jobation*. It looks like a derivative of *job*, but it is from *Job*: jobation is the sort of consolation that a Job's comforter provides. *Apocryphal* 'of doubtful authenticity' is often used in non-religious contexts as one of many ways of calling a man a liar. The Apocryphal Books of the Bible were excluded from the Biblical canon at the time of the Reformation. *Apocrypha* is from *apocrypha scripta* 'hidden writings'. *Maudlin* 'tearful' is from OFr *Maudelene*, borrowed through Latin from Greek *Magdalene*. Medieval and later painters generally depicted Mary Magdalene with eyes red and swollen with weeping. The choice of a proper name to form the basis of a common noun sometimes seems capricious. The question 'What did they *do* in Gomorrah?' was clearly prompted by the questioner's conviction that he knew what they did in Sodom; *sodomy* is recorded from the end of the thirteenth century.

Many proper names have passed into the language from literature. *Euphuism* derives its name from John Lyly's *Euphues: the Anatomy of Wit* (1578). Lyly wrote in a distinctive style, with a fondness for alliteration and classical allusions, that influenced many Elizabethan writers, including Shakespeare. *Benedick* 'a married man' is an allusion to Benedick in *Much Ado About Nothing*, who eventually marries Beatrice, his sparring partner through most of the play. The name of an editor of Shakespeare is preserved in *bowdlerise*. Thomas Bowdler was a physician who in 1818 published a *Family Shakespeare*, which omitted or modified those passages 'which cannot with propriety be read aloud in a family'. Defoe's *Robinson Crusoe* (1719) has given us *Man Friday*, sometimes meaning an aboriginal but also a cheerful, hard-working and versatile assistant. The phrase has become so much a part of our language that newspapers sometimes contain advertisements from would-be employers of *Girl Fridays*. Swift has given us two clumsy synonyms for 'large' and 'small' in *lilliputian* and *brobdingnagian* from the first two books of *Gulliver's Travels*. *Namby-pamby* 'weakly sentimental' is derived from the name of Ambrose Philips (d. 1749) in derision of the sentimentality of some of his poems. The word has survived while the poet has been forgotten; he was the object of scornful attacks by Pope. There are two examples of characters surviving longer than the work in which they occur in George Farquhar's *The Beaux' Stratagem* (1707): *Boniface* for an innkeeper and *Lady Bountiful* for a generous friend of the poor. Both terms are now rather old-fashioned. From other now-forgotten plays we have taken *Mrs Grundy* as a type of conventional propriety (Morton's *Speed the Plough*, 1798) and *a gay Lothario* 'a libertine' (Rowe's *Fair Penitent*, 1703). Mrs Malaprop in Sheridan's *The Rivals* (1775) has provided a name for a practice much older than Sheridan. A *malapropism* is the ludicrous result of confusion between two polysyllabic words similar in form.

When we reach the nineteenth century examples of the

creation of words involving literary allusions become more common. A *Collins* is a letter of thanks written by a guest after a visit. It is an allusion to chapter 22 of Jane Austen's *Pride and Prejudice*. Frankenstein is a character in Mary Shelley's novel of that name (1818) who creates a monster which gets out of control and murders its creator. *Frankenstein* comes to be used of anyone who creates a monstrous object that gets out of hand and, in popular use, it is often applied in error to the object so created. A *trilby* is a soft felt hat derived from Trilby as played on the stage rather than directly from George du Maurier's novel (1894). *Gilbertian* 'witty and fanciful with an element of paradox' is derived from the name of W. S. Gilbert (d. 1911), whose comic operas contained many fanciful situations.

The most important contributor of proper names to our vocabulary in the field of English literature was Dickens. 'What the Dickens?' is not an allusion to the novelist; *Dickens* was in use as a euphemism for the Devil as early as the sixteenth century. From the novels of Dickens we have *Gradgrind* 'a hard unimaginative utilitarian' (*Hard Times*), *Chadband* (*Bleak House*) and *Stiggins* (*Pickwick Papers*), both meaning 'a sanctimonius humbug', *Micawber* 'an impecunious optimist' (*David Copperfield*), *Pecksniff* 'an unctuous hypocrite' (*Martin Chuzzlewit*), *Scrooge* 'a curmudgeon' (*A Christmas Carol*) and *Uriah Heep* 'a hypocrite' (*David Copperfield*). Podsnap in *Our Mutual Friend* was a pompous upholder of the superiority of Englishmen to foreigners and a defender of 'the young person' against indelicacy; he has given us *Podsnappery*. Many partners in professional firms have profited by the example of Spenlow and Jorkins in *David Copperfield*, who shift responsibility for unwelcome decisions on to each other's shoulders. Three of the characters in *Oliver Twist* have passed into everyday language. Most people remember Oliver Twist as the boy who asked for more, although that was only one incident in a full and varied life. The other two characters in the novel who have contributed to our vocabulary are Bill Sikes 'a professional burglar' and Fagin 'keeper of a thieves' kitchen'. *Mrs Gamp* (*Martin Chuzzlewit*) is often used as a disrespectful term for a midwife, a heavy drinker or a gossipy old woman. She has rather surprisingly given her name as a slang term for an umbrella as a result of an incidental reference in chapter 19: 'Mrs Gamp had a large bundle with her, a pair of pattens, and a species of gig umbrella'. Her frequent references to her friend Mrs Harris, who never appears, have contributed Mrs Harris as a fictitious character comparable with Bunbury in Oscar Wilde's *The Importance of Being Earnest*. From these Dickensian names adjectives are sometimes formed, the best-known of which are *Micawberish* and *Pickwickian*.

Most people today, on hearing of 'the admirable Crichton', think of J. M. Barrie's play or Harrison Ainsworth's novel, but the term was applied in 1603 to James Crichton, a versatile Scot who excelled in disputation, athletics and the arts of war.

Words derived from the names of persons are usually from surnames, but *clerihew*, a piece of comic verse consisting of two rhymed couplets with lines of unequal length, is from the Christian name of Edmund Clerihew Bentley (d. 1956), a friend of G. K. Chesterton.

From literatures other than English proper names were adopted at an early date. *Machiavellian* 'cunning' is from Niccolo Machiavelli (d. 1527), a Florentine diplomat who wrote on history and the art of government. *Gargantuan* 'enormous' is derived from the name of a giant in the French *La Vie très horrifique du Grand Gargantua* (1534) by Rabelais, who has given us the adjective *Rabelaisian* to denote exuberant language and coarse humour. *Rodomontade* (often incorrectly spelt with initial *rh-*) 'vainglorious boasting' comes through French from the name of a braggart in Ariosto's *Orlando Furioso* (1516). *Quixotic* is well established in the language to denote anyone who resembles the Don Quixote of Cervantes in his generous and unworldly but self-deluding chivalry. From American literature we have *knickerbocker* and the comparatively recent *knickers* (*c.* 1880) from the name of the pretended author of Washington Irving's *History of New York* (1809) and *Babbitt* as the type of a complacent businessman from the novel of that name (1922) by Sinclair Lewis.

Words of any kind can tell us something about the history of the people who use them, but those derived from proper names are exceptionally informative; they can tell us about cultural history as well as historical events and the importance that they had for people living at the time. *Colossal* preserves the name of the Colossus of Rhodes, one of the seven wonders of the ancient world. *Magenta*, a brilliant crimson dye, preserves the name of the Battle of Magenta, which was fought in 1859, shortly before the dye was discovered, while *burnt sienna* and *Venetian red* preserve the names of other Italian cities. A *balaclava helmet*, a woollen covering for the head and neck, is a reminder of the intense cold suffered by soldiers fighting in the Crimean War. Battles have been especially liable to contribute words to our vocabulary. A *dumdum bullet*, a soft-nosed bullet that expands on impact, was first manufactured at the military station of Dum Dum near Calcutta. The verb *to maffick* is a back-formation to denote the scenes of popular rejoicing at the relief of Mafeking in 1900 after it had been besieged in the Boer War. *To lynch* 'to punish without adequate legal trial' is from Charles Lynch (d. 1796), who presided over an extra-legal court at the time of the American Revolution. A less drastic form of punishment is the *boycott*, a systematic refusal of social or commercial relations, which derives its name from Captain Charles Boycott, an Irish land agent who was given this treatment from 1880.

The name of a country or a people may be preserved in several different words, all going back ultimately to the same proper name. *Morocco leather* was originally made in Morocco. The French name for Morocco, Maroc, has given us *marocain*, a ribbed dress material resembling silk. The adjective *Moorish* has given us *morris dance*, perhaps so called because it was performed by dancers with blackened faces. Underlying most of the names of foreign nations introduced into English there is a strong element of xenophobia. *Welsh* is from OE *wēlisc*, a derivative of *wealh*, which meant both 'slave' and 'Celt'; it was related to Latin *Volcae*, the name of a Celtic tribe. Further evidence of the reduction of conquered races to slavery is provided by *slave*, from Medieval Latin *sclavus*, which meant both 'Slav' and 'slave'. A strong conviction that 'we are the people' underlies the use of the adjective *unEnglish* as a term of abuse. Many people no doubt think that this word is comparatively recent, a product of nineteenth-century self-satisfaction but it is first recorded in William Prynne's *Histriomastix* (1633). *Barbarian* is derived from Greek through Latin. Greek *barbaros* meant 'not Greek, foreign' and probably originally referred to speech. The Greeks said of an unfamiliar language that it sounded like *bar-bar*, just as an Englishman of today might say of a language that he couldn't understand that it was all *blah-blah*. The linguistic errors of the Athenian colonists of Soloi, in Cilicia, have given us *solecism*, and the difficulties that foreigners experience with unfamiliar sounds have given us *shibboleth*, a word whose use as a test is described in Judges 12.6. In Shakespeare's *Julius Caesar* I.2.287 *Greek* is used to denote unintelligible, high-flown language. Thieves' slang is described as *St Giles's Greek*, *pedlar's French* and *thieves' Latin*. *French leave* began to be used in the eighteenth century to denote the practice of leaving a social gathering without formally taking leave of one's hostess. In the Middle Ages *Dutch* was a general term used to denote all the Germanic languages; from about 1600 it began to have specific reference to the Netherlands. *Dutch courage* is courage induced by drinking; *to go Dutch* is to pay your own share of the expenses of a party; *double Dutch* means anything that is unintelligible. Most of the disparaging uses of the word arose from the seventeenth-century hostility between England and the Netherlands. We hear much today of *vandalism*, the wilful destruction of property. The word is derived from the Vandals, a Germanic people who ravaged Gaul, Spain and Rome in the fourth and fifth centuries.

Certain regions acquire special reputations. Gascons are thought to be boastful, so a *gasconade* means boastful talk. A *sybarite* is a luxurious and effeminate person, because the inhabitants of Sybaris in southern Italy had that reputation. *Corinthian* and *Ephesian* have both acquired the meaning 'debauchee', though both words have a rather literary flavour. *Bohemian* was at one time used in the sense 'gypsy'; the modern meaning of a socially unconventional person, especially an artist or a writer, was given to the word by Thackeray. The contribution of the Parthians to the English vocabulary has been picturesquely described by Anthony Powell:

> When, after nearly 500 years, the Parthians disappeared from history in about A.D. 225, they left – in their

traditional manner – a final arrow quivering in the language of Europe, the phrase 'a Parthian shot'.[1]

Arabia has given us *arab (horse)* and *(street) arab* beside derivatives like *arabesque* to denote the fancifully intertwined leaves that are common in Arabian decorative work. *Gum arabic* is a gum exuded by some kinds of acacia. *Lumber* 'old useless things' is from the Lombards of Northern Italy, who were active as bankers and pawnbrokers. The banking activities gave us the name Lombard Street in London; their pawnbroking left them with unredeemed pledges, often of little value, no better than lumber. The *polka* and *mazurka* were dances which became popular early in the nineteenth century. They are from Polish words meaning respectively 'a Polish woman' and 'a woman from the province of Mazovia'. The *polonaise* is a slow dance of Polish origin called by a French name. *Philistine* is an old word which has acquired a new meaning in modern times. It originally meant a member of a warlike race in Southern Palestine who fought against the Israelites. It was used in the students' slang of German universities to mean 'one who is not a student', hence 'an outsider'. Carlyle and Matthew Arnold introduced it into English, where it means a person with little interest in culture.

The misconception that caused the natives of North America to be called Red Indians has had a number of effects on our vocabulary. *Indian clubs* are so named because they resemble weapons used by North American Indians; *Indian corn* 'maize' was cultivated in America; *Indian file* 'single file' was a convenient way of walking through the North American forests; and *indiarubber* is made from the juice of trees that grow in South America. Another misconception is preserved in *India paper* and *Indian ink*, both of which were first made in China.

Places smaller than countries can acquire a reputation which is preserved in language. *Billingsgate* 'abusive language' is derived from the name of the fish-market held in that part of London from the thirteenth century, though the reputation of the porters for expressive language only goes back to the seventeenth. *Bedlam* is from the Hospital of Saint Mary of Bethlehem in London, which was converted into a lunatic asylum; the use of ***bedlam*** to mean a noisy and disorderly scene is a comment on the way in which such asylums were conducted. ***Blarney*** 'cajolery' is derived from Blarney, a village near Cork, where there is a castle incorporating a stone which is supposed to reward those who kiss it with the gift of loquacious prevarication, described more briefly in slang as the gift of the gab.

The names of persons which have given common nouns include a few large groups. Many names of flowers have been formed by the addition of the suffix *-ia* to the name of the botanist who discovered them or of someone that he wished to honour. We have ***aubrietia***, named after Claude Aubriet (d. 1743), a French painter of animals and flowers, ***banksia*** after Sir Joseph Banks (d. 1820), an English naturalist who accompanied Cook on his voyage round the world, ***begonia*** after Michel Bégon (d. 1710), an administrator in the French West Indies, ***dahlia*** after the Swedish botanist Anders Dahl (d. 1789), a friend of Linnaeus, ***eschscholtzia*** after Johann Friedrich von Eschscholtz (d. 1831), a German botanist, ***forsythia*** after the English botanist William Forsyth (d. 1804), ***lobelia*** after the Flemish botanist Matthias de Lobel (d. 1616), ***magnolia*** named by Linnaeus in honour of Pierre Magnol (d. 1715), a French physician, and ***wistaria*** after Caspar Wistar (d. 1818), an American anatomist. Knowledge of the etymology is a safeguard against the frequent misspelling of ***fuchsia***; it was named after Leonhard Fuchs (d. 1566), a German botanist. Sometimes a surname is applied to a fruit without change, as in ***baldwin***, the name of a kind of apple first grown by Loammi Baldwin (d. 1807), an American engineer, or it may form an element of a compound, as in ***loganberry***, a cross between a blackberry and a raspberry discovered in 1881 by James Harvey Logan in California.

Names of diseases may come from those who suffered from them or from those who tried to cure them. A ***masochist***, who takes pleasure in pain inflicted on himself, is so called because the Austrian novelist Leopold von Sacher-Masoch (d. 1895) described a sufferer from this perversion. The word is often used light-heartedly of anyone who is 'a glutton for punishment'. ***Sadism***, the sexual perversion marked by cruelty, derives its name from the Count de Sade (d. 1814), who wrote several novels and plays.

The word is often used as a heightened variant of 'cruelty' without sexual connotations. *Bilharzia* is a genus of parasites in human blood which causes the disease bilharziasis; it was named after Theodor Bilharz, the German physician who discovered the parasite in 1851. Diseases named after the medical men who discovered them include *Bright's disease*, *Hodgkin's disease* and *Parkinson's disease*. Those named after saints include *St Vitus' dance* and *St Anthony's fire*, another name for erysipelas. Stages in the history of medicine are recorded in *galvanism*, electricity developed by chemical action used for medical purposes in the nineteenth century, derived from the name of Luigi Galvani (d. 1798), an Italian physiologist, and *mesmerism*, a hypnotic state produced by the exercise of somebody else's will-power, derived from the name of Friedrich Anton Mesmer (d. 1815), an Austrian physicist.

Products have often preserved the names of their inventors. *Bakelite* is a synthetic resin invented by a Flemish chemist Leo Hendrik Baekeland (d. 1944). *Bessemer* is steel made by decarbonising melted pig-iron, a process invented by Sir Harry Bessemer (d. 1898). The name of Samuel Plimsoll (d. 1898) is preserved in two quite different connections. He gave his name to a rubber-soled canvas sports-shoe and he was the promoter of the Merchant Shipping Act of 1876, which required that all British merchant vessels should have a load-line to show whether they were overloaded. A *chesterfield*, a sofa with padded seat, back and ends, was named after a nineteenth-century Earl of Chesterfield, not the more famous earl of the eighteenth century. The *bunsen burner* is named after Robert Wilhelm von Bunsen (d. 1899), the German physicist; the *Davy lamp*, a miner's safety lamp, is named after Sir Humphry Davy (d. 1829), the English chemist; and the *zeppelin* is named after Ferdinand, Count Zeppelin (d. 1917), the German airman. Printers have given their names to types which they designed. *Baskerville* type was designed by John Baskerville (d. 1775) of Birmingham, *Caslon* by William Caslon (d. 1766), and *Clarendon* was named after the Clarendon Press at Oxford, which profited from the sale of the Earl of Clarendon's *History of the Rebellion* (1702–4). Firearms have been named after their inventors, giving *gatling* (in slang shortened to *gat*) from Dr

Richard Gatling (d. 1903), ***maxim*** from Sir Hiram Maxim (d. 1916), and *lewis* from Isaac Newton Lewis (d. 1931), an American army officer. Less often the name of a gun is derived from a place. ***Bren gun*** is a blend of Brno, in Czechoslovakia, where the gun was first made, and Enfield, near London, where it was manufactured after the patent was bought by the British Government. Two methods of communication preserve the names of their inventors. The *morse* code, consisting of arrangements of dots and dashes to represent letters in telegraphy, was invented by an American electrician, Samuel Morse (d. 1872). ***Braille***, a method of reading for the blind based upon variations in the positions of six raised dots, was invented by Louis Braille (d. 1852), himself blind from the age of three, who became a teacher of the blind.

An outline history of electrical engineering is provided by the names of various kinds of electrical units, which show how international science has become. The most familiar are *volt*, the unit of electromotive force, from Count Allesandro Volta (d. 1827), the Italian physicist, *watt*, with its derivative *kilowatt*, the unit of power, from James Watt (d. 1819), the Scottish engineer, and *amp*, the unit of electrical current, from André Ampère (d. 1836), the French scientist. Others in less general use are *ohm*, the unit of resistance, from Georg Simon Ohm (d. 1854), the German physicist, and *coulomb*, the unit of electric charge, from Charles Augustin de Coulomb (d. 1806), the French engineer and physicist.

The article invented may be quite simple but, if it satisfies a need, its name spreads and becomes a household word. *Sandwich* is derived from the name of the fourth Earl of Sandwich (d. 1792), a gambler who once spent twenty-four hours at the gaming-table without any meal except slices of cold meat between two slices of toast. Articles of dress may derive their names from famous men who wore them. A *raglan*, a kind of overcoat without shoulder-seams, was named after the first Baron Raglan (d. 1855), commander of the British forces in the Crimean War. The leader of the Charge of the Light Brigade at Balaclava was the seventh Earl of Cardigan, and he gave his name to the *cardigan*, a knitted woollen jacket. *Wellingtons*, rubber waterproof boots reaching the knee, were named after the first Duke of

Wellington (d. 1852); in dialects the word is affectionately shortened to *wellies*.

Place-names have been as productive as personal names in their contributions to our vocabulary. Wines tend to be named after the places from which they first came, and there are sometimes law-suits to establish whether a region can keep exclusive rights in the use of a name that has become world-famous. *Chablis* is made near the small town of Chablis in the *département* of Yonne, France; *Chambertin* was named after a Burgundian vineyard eight miles from Dijon; *champagne* was originally the wine of Champagne, a province of eastern France; *burgundy* is from the ancient province of Burgundy; *sherry* originally came form Xeres (now Jerez) in Andalusia, and *Amontillado* from the hilly district round Montilla in Spain; *Benedictine* takes its name from the Benedictine monks of Fécamp in Normandy, and *Chartreuse* from La Grande Chartreuse, the Carthusian monastery near Grenoble. *Cognac* is now used loosely to denote any French brandy; it was first applied to brandy from Cognac in western France. *Bourbon* whisky distilled from maize and rye takes its name from Bourbon County in Kentucky, where it was first made. Holland has given its name to *Hollands*, a kind of gin made from rye; it owes its final *-s* to its origin in *hollandsch genever* 'Dutch gin'. Two cocktails derive their names from New York place-names: a *Manhattan* from Manhattan Island and a *Bronx* from the northern suburb of the Bronx.

Different kinds of cheese are named after the places where they were first made, which are sometimes small and known chiefly because of the reputation of their cheese. *Gorgonzola* is from the town of that name in Lombardy; *Parmesan* is from a French adjective meaning 'of Parma'; *Roquefort* is from a town in south-western France; *Camembert* is from a village of that name near Argentan in France; *Stilton* is from a parish in Huntingdonshire, *Cheddar* from a village in Somerset, and so on through a long list of cheese-producing regions.

Of other foods a brief selection may be given. *Finnan haddock* is derived from either Findon or Findhorn, both of which are seaside villages in Scotland. In chapter 26 of *The*

Antiquary (1816) Scott says that Findhorn haddocks are haddocks smoked with green wood. A *sardine* is a fish found off the coast of Sardinia. A *bantam* is a small breed of fowl which was thought to come from Bantam in Java. The word is used, with some exaggeration, as an element of *bantam-weight* to denote a category of boxers intermediate between feather-weight and fly-weight. Sometimes the origin of a food may be disguised by sound-changes, as in *peach*, from OFr *pesche*, from Latin *persicum (malum)* 'Persian fruit'.

From food and drink to clothes. The first meaning of *milliner* was 'an inhabitant of Milan'. From that it came to mean a dealer in articles made in Milan, such as bonnets, ribbons and gloves. Many textile fabrics are named after their supposed place of origin. *Calico* is a cotton cloth from Calicut in India; *cashmere* is made from the soft wool of a Kashmir goat; *nankeen* is a yellow cotton cloth named after the Chinese city of Nanking; *denims* incorporates a preposition and is from the town of Nîmes in France; *jeans* is from the Middle English form of the place-name Genoa, where this kind of cotton cloth was first manufactured. *Duffle*, a coarse woollen cloth, used most often in *duffle coat*, a hooded overcoat with toggle fastenings instead of buttons, is from Duffel in Belgium. Other commercial products are named after places: *malacca* is a walking-stick of a rich brown colour from Malacca in Malaysia; *manil(l)a* is the name of a cigar and a kind of stiff paper from Manila, the capital of the Philippines; *damask* and *damson plums* are both from Damascus.

Breeds of dogs are named after their real or supposed place of origin, which may be in almost any part of the world. The *Bedlington* takes its name from a town in Northumberland, the *Skye terrier* from the Isle of Skye, the *Airedale* from a Yorkshire river. From abroad we have the *Afghan hound*, the *Alsatian* from Alsace, the *Dalmatian* from Yugoslavia, the *Pekinese* from China, the *Saluki* from Saluq, an ancient city of southern Arabia, and the *Samoyed* from Siberia. The *St Bernard* life-saving dog was named after the Hospice of the Great St Bernard, a pass in the Alps. Less obvious is the *spaniel*, from OFr *espagnol*.

CHAPTER FOUR

Dialect and Slang

It is not always easy to distinguish between dialects and other varieties of English, such as slang and register. The essential difference between a dialect and a register is that the former is used habitually by a group of people, while the latter depends on the occasion when it is used, formal or informal, for business or for pleasure. The difficulty in distinguishing between the two varieties arises because a group may be either permanent or temporary. If a number of doctors get together to discuss a patient's condition, they are likely to use a lot of technical terms. Are they using their occupational dialect or a register? If the sort of language that they employ is that used by doctors on all occasions, it is an occupational dialect; if it is used only on certain occasions, it is best regarded as a register.

Since register depends upon occasion, it follows that it is constantly changing. A man may use a dozen or more registers in the course of a day without any feeling of incongruity or inconsistency. Indeed, a sense of incongruity would arise if he were to fail to adapt his language to changing circumstances. The divergence between the registers of written English and those of everyday life becomes clear if we analyse the language of conversation. Such language does not need to be explicit, because the speakers rely on the context within which the conversation is taking place. A tape-recording of a conversation is often puzzling or ambiguous because it isolates speech from its context of such things as gesture and facial expression. There are many inarticulate mumbles, and sentences are often incomplete, tailing off into silence as the speaker becomes conscious that he is not keeping the attention of his hearers. If the participants know each other well, their recorded conversation becomes even more obscure, because they are able to take more for granted. There are brief allusions to jokes and previous events and conversations well known to both participants but baffling to a stranger. It is of the essence of conversation that it should move quickly from one subject to another, and such swift movements add to the obscurity. Incomplete sentences, deviations from traditional grammar and hesitation are so normal in conversation that we tend to distrust anyone who does not indulge in these practices; we say that he talks like a book or that he knows all the answers. Parentheses are more common in conversation than in written English, since the speaker has no time to remove irrelevancies. Other features of the language of conversation are the frequency of contracted verbal forms like *I'll* and of overused words like *got*. The vocabulary of conversation is generally simple. When unfamiliar words are used, they tend to be played down by hesitation or an apologetic 'you know', 'I mean' or 'sort of'. Slang is tolerated and there are naturally many colloquialisms like *a bit*.

The deliberate use of the wrong variety of English is fairly common. The use of the dialect of a higher social class than one's own is the mark of an unskilful social climber; the deliberate use of a substandard dialect is generally a joke or a pleasantry. When Winston Churchill was Prime Minister in 1952 he sent for Reginald Maudling to offer him the post of Parliamentary Secretary to the Ministry of Civil Aviation. Maudling did not come at once, so the message was repeated by a senior messenger from the Whip's Office, who said 'The boss wants you, sharpish like'. (*Daily Telegraph*, 15 February 1979). The deliberately inappropriate register toned down the peremptory nature of the summons.

The most striking feature of the English dialect vocabulary is its richness within certain fields. The selective nature of those fields tells us a good deal about the character of dialect speakers. Mrs E. M. Wright reports[1] that the *English Dialect Dictionary* records approximately 1350 words meaning to give a person a thrashing, 1300 ways of telling a person he is a fool and about 1050 terms for a slattern. Terms for a fool include such satisfying words as *chuffin head*, *gapus*, *goostrumnoodle*, *mee-maw*, *ning-nang*, *yawney*, *yonnack*, *goffeny goavey* and *dunder-headed slinpole*. Words for a slattern include *daffock*, *dawps*, *drazzle-drozzle*, *hagmahush*, *lirrox*, *moggy*, *slommocks* and *wally-draigle*. There are very few dialect words to denote a wise man or a good housewife. It is clear that outspokenness is a characteristic of dialect speakers, especially in the North, which is the part of the country where regional dialects are best preserved. The richness of the vocabulary is all the more remarkable when we remember the taciturnity of many dialect speakers.

The quarrelsomeness that is revealed by analysis of the vocabulary is confirmed when we look at some common dialect phrases. 'We'll begin as we mean to go on' is not in itself a declaration of hostile intent, but it is usually the prelude to a further declaration that is distinctly hostile. The tiresome demand for repetition that is implicit in the frequent use of the word 'pardon' is generally accepted as one of the minor trials of life, but if addressed to a dialect speaker it is liable to meet with the robust reply 'I don't boil my cabbages twice'.

The impression of hostility that is gained on the first contact with dialect speakers is misleading. It is an over-reaction resulting from a hatred of insincerity and of the too-ready expression of friendly feelings. When the initial reserve is broken down the dialect speaker is capable of strong friendly emotions, which find their expression in dialect poetry. The chief impression that dialect verse makes on a reader who is not familiar with it is one of excessive sentimentality. The emotion that is most often expressed is strong family feeling, found, for example, in Samuel Laycock's 'Welcome, bonny brid', written to welcome a baby born during the Cotton Famine. A linguistic expression of this strong family feeling is the common dialect practice of inserting 'our' before the name of a member of the family, though one motive is no doubt the practical one of distinguishing our Jack from the many other Jacks in the village. It is sometimes used as a form of address, and a sister might address her brother as 'our Bill'.

The northern dialects are spoken in areas which were covered by the Danelaw, and there are resemblances between the grim humour of characters in the Icelandic sagas and that of northern dialect speakers. Two instances of this grim humour occurred during the Second World War. A sailor, who had the task of rowing a visitor out to a ship, gave him ironical encouragement when he was about to jump from the boat to the ship: 'Aye, go on, jump it. It's nobbut a couple o' jumps'. The second instance occurred when an idler was watching a man digging with a pick-axe round an unexploded bomb. He could not resist the urge to ask a silly question: 'What would happen if you were to hit it?' The reply was in the best northern tradition: 'You'd lose t'pick'.

It is not always possible to find a good reason for the large number of dialect synonyms. A familiar example is the wide variety of different words used to denote the weakest pig of a litter in different parts of country.[2] Peter Wright[3] records that a man who unloads fish at the quayside in the early morning is called a *maggy*, a *lumper*, a *bobber* or a *dock-walloper*. Whenever we find a large number of apparent synonyms, we have to be prepared to find that they are not exact synonyms; they appear so to us because of our ignorance of the way of life of the people who use them. Peter Wright points out (p. 162) that there are many dialect synonyms for 'alley', such as *troughing*, *tewer*, *smoot*, *giggle-gaggle* and *dranjey*. Two common north-country words to express similar ideas are *snicket* and *ginnel*, but these two words are shibboleths which northerners use to distinguish those with a thorough knowledge from those with only a smattering. Both are narrow passages between houses, but a ginnel has a roof with rooms above it whereas a snicket is open to the sky. The term *snicket* was originally used to denote the latch on a gate; it then came to be used for the gate itself and eventually it denoted the footpath or alley to which the gate gave access.

Standard English and the dialects go back to a common source. Some words that have passed out of use in standard English have survived in frequent use in dialects. A few short, learned words have, rather surprisingly, found their way into dialects. For example, *nous*, a term used by Greek philosophers in the sense 'mind, intellect', occurs in dialects with the meaning 'common sense, gumption', perhaps through the medium of students' slang. Another Greek loan-word *rhizome*, a botanical term meaning a subterranean stem, occurs in Yorkshire dialects in the expression *not a rhizome* 'not a scrap'. The borrowing is understandable: dialect-speaking farmers have a good deal to do with rhizomes.

Once the divergence between the vocabularies of dialects and those of standard English was established, a two-way traffic set in. The words borrowed from standard English into dialects call for little comment; virtually all dialect speakers have some contact with standard English, and they would see nothing remarkable in an addition to the large number of words common to both forms of speech. The borrowings from dialects into standard English are more noticeable. Examples of northern words that have passed into standard English are *croon*, *eerie*, *flunkey*, *gloaming*, *rampage* and *scunner*. Other words, like *daft* and *gormless*, have not been completely assimilated into the standard language; their meanings are understood fairly generally but the words are still regarded as dialectal. Some words introduced from dialects in the nineteenth century were revivals. *Shunt* is found in early Middle English but it survived only as an obscure dialect word until the development of railways brought it into more general use. *Trolley* was a Suffolk word which became more general for similar reasons. Some words denote scenery that is to be found especially in the north, like the Lakeland *beck*, *fell*, *ghyll* and *tarn*, which are common in the works of Wordsworth and other Lake poets. Some Scots words have entered the vocabulary of the nursery; words like *bairn*, *cosy* and *wee* may have been introduced by Scotswomen who had the care of children. Other Scots words which have become standard are *astir*, *eldritch*, *fey*, *galore*, *glamour*, *gruesome*, *pawky*, *pony*, *slithery*, *slogan*, *sprint*, *toddle*, *uncanny*, *warlock*, *wizened* and *wraith*.[4]

Some words have almost disappeared in standard English but have survived in dialects. These include *bide* 'wait', *dree* 'suffer', *fain* 'glad', *nesh* 'soft', *speer* 'ask' and *thole* 'endure'. *Don* (for *do on*) and *doff* (for *do off*) are common in dialects, but in standard English they are bookish or poetic words.

Many dialect words are doublets of words which are common in standard English, such as *raid* beside *road*. Both of the words thus linked may be dialectal. The one thing that most of us know about a mickle is that it takes a lot of them to make a muckle, but *mickle* and *muckle* are dialectal variants of the same word, from ON *mikell*. *COD* suggests that the original form of the proverb was 'Many a little (*or* pickle) makes a mickle' and that the form *mickle* has been substituted in error.

Some dialect words are loan-words, borrowed into dialects but not into standard English. The words thus borrowed include several Scots words taken from French, such as *douce*, *dour* and *fash*. Some are compounds of common English words, like *witchert* 'wet-shod' and *winter-hedge* 'clothes-horse'.

Since the word 'dialect' is sometimes used pejoratively, anyone who applies it to an important variety of English is liable to be accused of trying to pick a quarrel, but it seems proper to regard British and American English as dialects of one language that it is convenient to call English, though some people prefer to call it Anglo-American. The justification for this term is that it recognises the importance of the largest group of speakers of the language; the chief drawback is that it omits to mention groups in various parts of the world who share the same language. The term 'English' may be preferred on the grounds of conciseness and on historical grounds. It is important to get away from the conception of dialect that it involves deviation from a norm. It is only when an Englishman travels that he realises how insular some of his idioms are. *Top hole* 'excellent' is a feature of old-fashioned class dialect in British English; it is more likely to be used by men than by women, by the elderly than by the young, and by the upper classes, but it is distinctly British English and, if used at all in America, it is most likely to be to indicate a stage stereotype of an Englishman. *Stone* as a measure of weight and *fortnight* as a measure of time are in such general use in British English that the average Englishman has no idea that they are not equally general in America.

The semantics of dialects is a neglected study, but it is worth the attention of those who come into contact with dialect speakers. A visitor caused serious offence by admiring the freshness of a farmer's daughter; he did not know that in the local dialect *fresh* meant 'unchaste'. Logan Pearsall Smith[5] tells how a countryman was saved from a heavy sentence in a court of law when it was explained that the *neife* with which he admitted that he had struck a neighbour was not a knife but his fist. The same author reports that he was in the chair when a rustic orator declared that he and his friends had no wish to see Tariff Reformers 'fawnicating about the village'. This remark was frequently repeated and applauded; the lack of protest was explained when he found that in the village the word *fawnicate* meant no more than to behave in a deceitful or intriguing way. Other semantic surprises recorded by Smith, especially affecting words of foreign origin, are that in some Scottish dialects *moniment* means 'fool' and *catastrophes* are pieces of broken china. In other dialects *comical* means 'bad-tempered' or 'ill', a *hypocrite* is an invalid, *jometry* means 'magic', *logaram* and *logic* mean 'balderdash', *miraculous* means 'very drunk', a *pedigree* is a rigmarole, *spiritual* means 'angry' and *stagnate* means 'astonish'. Words used for emphasis or to express strong emotion are particularly liable to undergo changes of meaning. Such words are *audacious*, *desperate*, *fell*, *furious*, *heinous*, *lamentable*, *miserable* and *perfumed*.

We sometimes find close parallels between the development of meaning of a word in dialects and standard English, as, for example, in the intensive use of *right*. To say that we know something 'right well' is archaic, while to use titles like 'Right Honourable' or 'Right Reverend' is rather formal, but this use of *right* is familiar to dialect speakers, who, when deeply moved, will describe somebody as 'a reight grand chap'.

The use of technical terms is the most easily recognisable feature of a register, as it is of an occupational dialect. Some words begin as the technical terms of a small group, but then pass into general use. In spite of their length and obviously learned origin, such words as *appendicitis*, *photography* and *haemorrhage* are no longer technical terms. When technical terms pass into general use, they sometimes undergo a change of meaning that disguises their origin. We speak of an activity at which anyone is especially proficient as his *forte* and, if he has a weakness, we call it a *foible*. Both words are from the technical language of fencing. The forte is the part of a sword-blade from the hilt to the middle and its name is derived from the French adjective *fort* 'strong'; the foible is the part of the blade from the middle to the tip and its name, as a doublet of *feeble*, is a suitable one to denote weakness of character.

Technical terms have played a large part in the extension of the English vocabulary. Judged only by the number of words, they occupy the major part of most lists of neologisms, but most of them never really take root in the language. They are there to be used when specialists are talking among themselves, but they remain unknown to the man in the street. A few exceptions, like *orbit* and *zenith*, have been in the language for some time, borrowed from the science of astronomy, and modern inventions, like television and the internal combustion engine, have had such an impact on our everyday life that each invention has carried with it a group of technical terms that are on everybody's lips, though many of those who use them have only a vague idea of their meaning. Some of these words become vogue words. Science and technology today have a prestige value, and therefore many people feel that it adds to the impressiveness of what they are saying if they can drag in an occasional reference to a *matrix* or a *parameter*.

It may be that we have grown so used to technical terms about whose meaning we are uncertain that we are learning to get along without much exact knowledge. James Woodhouse, the headmaster of Rugby, reported to a school speech day audience that he had seen an advertisement which read:

> Wanted. Man to work on nuclear fissionable isotope molecular reactive counters and three phase cyclotronic uranium synthesisers. No experience necessary.[6]

The fondness for technical terms is no new thing. Far-reaching and improbable conclusions have been drawn from Shakespeare's use of the technical terms of a wide range of subjects; it is rash to conclude that a man who uses a lot of legal terms must have been a lawyer.

Some technical terms come into use because of the extension of the boundaries of knowledge, others because of a search for greater precision in the use of terms already known. It is inadequate to describe a disease by naming one of its symptoms, and terms like *fever*, *consumption*, *growing pains* or *a wasting disease* tend to be replaced by more specific terms. It is coming to be realised that words like *cancer* and *rheumatism* each denote a whole group of diseases which will no doubt in time receive separate names. We often find pairs of terms, one learned and the other popular, with the same meaning: *myopia* and *short-sightedness*, *hernia* and *rupture*, *tetanus* and *lockjaw*. The loan-words are gaining ground over the native terms and are favoured by hypochondriacs, who find it easier to gain sympathy for a virus infection than a common cold. The coining of technical terms from Greek elements can result in the creation of very long words, and these are sometimes cut down to a more convenient size by the use of initials, such as *DDT* for *dichlorodiphenyl-trichloroethane* and *PVC* for *polyvinyl chloride*.

Many people dislike technical terms because their use makes it immediately obvious to the reader without technical knowledge what a lot of things he doesn't know, and technical terms which change frequently are undoubtedly a nuisance. Those who lay claim to special knowledge sometimes antagonise their readers by saying that something or other has been done 'for technical reasons' (i.e. for reasons that the reader is not bright enough to understand) but, properly used, technical terms serve a useful purpose. Richard Hoggart has pointed out two reasons why they are sometimes necessary:

> Specialists do need specialist languages for at least two good reasons: as forms of shorthand to speed up discussions between themselves and as safeguards against their analyses being misinterpreted because some of their words might be read in more than one sense. This is especially necessary in social-scientific studies; their language must be so far as possible cleansed of the ambiguities of subjective readings.[7]

It is when technical language is used by people who are not specialists that the trouble begins. Then technical language becomes jargon, and attacks on technical language should be directed at its excessive or inappropriate use. Such language would not flourish as it does unless it made a strong appeal to some readers as well as writers. Kenneth Hudson gives a salutary reminder:

> One can write or speak absolute rubbish, but, if it is the right kind of rubbish, it can bring one an abundance of friends and allies among people who habitually use the same variety of nonsense language. There are no stronger

> links than those between sufferers from the same illness, even when that illness is madness. To the irreverent layman, 'each component of a response-sequence provides sensory feedback in the form of response-produced kinesthetic and proproceptive cues' sounds like pompous piffle, which indeed it is, but to a fellow psychologist or sociologist it indicates a friend, someone with his head and heart in the right place, someone worth knowing. For the initiates it is rank-closing, masonic language, with no power to stimulate those who live outside the group.[8]

Technical terms are needed to denote new applications of science to everyday life, such as *sellotape*. Like the Anglo-Saxons, who sometimes used word formation from native elements to express the new ideas introduced by Christianity, we use compound words to denote the new ideas introduced by technology, as in *non-stick frying-pan*.

Every art or trade has its own technical vocabulary, and a few of the words, which denote objects in common use, gain a wider currency. The use of technical terms saves time; it is much quicker to name a process than to describe it. Sometimes, as in legal language, precise definition is essential and in order to secure it we are willing to sacrifice such virtues as conciseness. For the purpose of scientific description we need a language that is exact. Haunting rhythms are unnecessary and the associations of ideas which contribute so much to the appeal of the language of poetry are a nuisance to the scientist. In poetry vagueness may be a virtue in leaving much to the imagination of the reader, but to the scientist it is a curse. He is not trying to arouse emotions or to present beauty but to make himself understood with as little margin for error as possible. The language of science has no use for polysemy or semantic development. The scientist needs to be confident that his hearer will attach exactly the same meaning to a word that he himself gives to it. Henry Bradley pointed out that this is the reason why a scientist often finds it necessary to coin a new word:

> it is often a positive disadvantage that a scientific word should suggest too obtrusively its etymological meaning. A term which is taken from a foreign language, or formed

> out of foreign elements, can be rigidly confined to the meaning expressed in its definition; a term of native formation cannot be so easily divested of misleading popular associations.[9]

Scientific terms can acquire emotional associations when they pass into popular use. T. H. Savory[10] points out that *peroxide* was originally a scientific word with no emotive content, but hydrogen peroxide bleaches hair, and the opinion once held of women who used it for that purpose gave a derogatory sense to *peroxide blonde*. Similarly he points out that *atomic* has acquired associations with terror and destruction because of the atomic bomb.

Examples of technical vocabulary will be given here from many different spheres of human activity, from science and philosophy, from sport and activities like sailing that are a sport for some and an occupation for others, from occupations and trade and from professions like medicine, law and diplomacy. To limit an enormous field to manageable proportions, we shall confine ourselves to words which began as technical terms but which, for good or ill, have passed into more general use.

Much of the language of psychology and sociology has passed into general use as a series of clichés like 'behaviour patterns' and 'basic insecurity' and words like *ambivalence* and *motivation*. These are unfamiliar words used to denote familiar ideas. In botany and zoology technical terms of Latin or Greek origin have been used in the hope of imposing a system that can be internationally understood, but the attempt has brought with it problems, as is clear from the lament of a naturalist:

> The scientific names for animals are in an almost incredible confusion owing to recent well-intentioned efforts to apply world-wide rules intended to standardize them. So far the chief result has been to replace many names, long known and universally understood, by others laboriously excavated from obsolete literature or evolved from the fertile minds of systematists.[11]

Much of the confusion arises from the existence of two methods of nomenclature: the binomial, consisting of two terms, the first being the name of the genus and the second that of the species, and the trinomial, which adds a third term indicating the subspecies or variety. There is some repetition since, in the trinomial system, every name must have three terms, either by duplication or addition. Even in the binomial system the English black rat or plague-rat becomes *Rattus rattus.*[12] A single plant may have many quite different local names, and such diversity presents obvious difficulties to the scientist, although the poetic and imaginative local names may appeal to the layman. The foxglove, for example, has such names as *fairy thimbles*, *witches' thimbles*, *bloody man's fingers*, *dead man's bells*, *flop-a-dock*, *poppy-dock* and *pop-guns.*[13] A scientist does not need to be a very profound classical scholar to remember the meanings of elements which frequently recur in scientific compound words. An object may have more than one name: a long scientific name for international currency and one or more local names for popular use. The length of scientific terms is no bar to their easy comprehension so long as they are made up of familiar elements. There can be important differences between the meanings of a technical term in scientific and popular use. To the layman *salt* means one particular chemical, sodium chloride, but to the chemist it is a generic term for a chemical compound in which one element of an acid, hydrogen, has been replaced in whole or in part by another, and common salt is only one of many chemicals that answer to this description.

Some long but familiar words originally belonged to the technical language of philosophy, but they have passed into general use with a change of meaning. A *predicament* was originally a thing predicated, especially in Aristotle's ten categories; it now generally denotes an unpleasant or dangerous situation. *Nonentity* originally denoted a state of non-existence, then a non-existent thing; it is now used to denote a person so unimportant that he might just as well not be there at all. *Non-existent* itself is a philosophical term that we now use in more general contexts. A *premise* is still used in logic to denote a previous statement from which another is inferred. In the plural it became a legal term to denote aforesaid matters, which were often houses or lands. It thus acquired its usual modern sense of a building with the ground on which it stands. *Quality* and *quantity* were originally philosophical terms, derivatives of Latin *qualis* 'of what kind' and *quantus* 'how much'. Less familiar today is *quiddity*, a derivative of Latin *quid* 'what', originally meaning the characteristic quality of anything, what makes it what it is, but when the teachings of the medieval schoolmen became unpopular, it came to mean 'quibble'.

The four elements were in classical times thought to be earth, air, fire and water. A need was felt for a term to denote a fifth substance which permeated space and filled the interstices between particles of matter. In Medieval Latin this was known as *quinta essentia* 'the fifth essence'; *quintessence* has come to mean the most important component part or manifestation of a quality.

Astrology has given us *disaster*, originally meaning the unfavourable aspect of a star, *predominant*, a word applied to a planet which is powerful at a particular moment, *horoscope*, a diagram showing the position of the planets at a particular time, especially at a person's birth, and adjectives, such as *saturnine*, *jovial*, *mercurial* and *lunatic*, denoting the supposed characteristics of those born or acting under the influence of particular heavenly bodies.

Every sport has its own vocabulary and, since sport arouses wide interest, much of this has passed into our everyday language. Thus we get *bias* from bowls, 'to track down', 'at fault', 'at a loss' and 'in at the death' from hunting, *well-groomed* from horsemanship, 'to cross swords' from fencing, 'below the belt' from boxing, and 'to wrestle with a problem'. Cock-fighting, once more highly esteemed than it is today, has given terms like *crestfallen* and *well-heeled* and idioms like 'to fight shy' and 'to show the white feather', since white feathers in a gamecock's tail are a sign of bad breeding. From sports that are no longer popular we have 'full tilt', 'to tilt at' and 'to break a lance' from jousting, and 'to miss the mark' from archery. Horse-racing, dicing and card games have a high proportion of slang in their technical vocabularies. Racing has given 'dark horse', 'also ran' and *welsher*; card games have produced slang phrases like 'to pass the buck' and 'to ante up', and more formal expressions like those that we use when we say that we are within an ace of collapse or that we are playing with the cards close to the chest or that our opponent has something up his sleeve. A 'poker face' is one that does not betray emotion, and it is a useful asset in a game which depends largely on bluff. The name of the game *nap* is derived from Napoleon. 'To go nap' is to attempt the highest score, hence to aim at the best. 'To nap' is to bet all one's money on one horse with the audacity that Napoleon showed when he concentrated on one point of attack. Technical terms can pass from one sphere to another. 'Blue chips' are now thought of as belonging to the language of the stock exchange to denote shares that are a reliable investment without being as safe as gilt-edged; originally they were high-value counters used in poker.

Nautical terms are particularly liable to be misused when they pass into everyday speech. Seafarers think that their meaning is so obvious that they find it hard to explain them to landlubbers without using more technical terms. A term may acquire a completely different meaning in general use. This has happened to *leeway*, the technical meaning of which is described by Philip Howard:

> *Leeway* means the lateral drift downward, that is to leeward, of course made involuntarily by a ship, especially a sailing ship, which is trying not to go down wind. A vessel can make a lot of *leeway* if a strong cross tide is running, or if her keel is not long enough or deep enough to give her a good grip of the water and hold her up to the wind. It can be extremely dangerous. Even when it is not, it is entirely undesirable. There are no circumstances in which it is a good thing.
>
> Yet the word now occurs constantly in landlubbers' generalized discourse as if *leeway* were something to be desired, like a breathing-space. It is used as if it meant a respectable margin for error instead of a damaging failure to adhere to the course intended. If people must put on bogus nautical airs, the correct word for manoeuvre or margin of error is 'sea-room'.[14]

Other technical terms that have passed from nautical into everyday use include *headway*, *to founder* and *to scuttle* and phrases like 'under way', 'taken aback', 'to steer clear of' and 'to weather the storm'. The first element of *starboard* (OE *stēorbord*) is related to *steer*, and the word came into use because sailors, when right-handed, steered boats with a paddle over the right-hand side. *Larboard* (ME *ladebord*) owed its form in part to *starboard*, but the resemblance in form could lead to dangerous confusion and it has generally been replaced by *port*.

Language is quick to meet the needs of new inventions. The word *television* was recorded as long ago as 1907, and the names of the two branches of broadcasting do not remain stable. *Radio* and *sound radio* are replacing *wireless*, and *TV* and the colloquial *telly* are replacing *television*. Radio and television have made such an impact on our lives that they have inevitably affected our language, and those who work in these fields have developed their own technical language, including much slang. The credits displayed after a television programme often include the name of the *dubbing mixer*, an occupation of which most of us were unaware until a few years ago, and even now many of us would have difficulty in saying just what it is that he does. We are all familiar with the noun *commercial* to denote an advertising interlude, and most of us know that a *DJ* is a *disc jockey*, who introduces gramophone records interspersed with friendly patter. Mario Pei[15] mentions other examples, used especially in America, but also from time to time in Great Britain. *Dead air* is a period of silence; an *inherited audience* is one left over from a preceding popular programme, consisting of listeners who are too tired to switch off their sets; a *creeper* is an actor who moves too near to the microphone; *to cue-bite* is to begin one's speech before the previous speaker has finished; and a *mike* is a microphone. *Soap opera* for a radio daytime serial is of American origin; the name was given because programmes of this kind were extensively sponsored by soap manufacturers. Some theatrical terms, like *ad-libbing* 'improvising', have been transferred to radio.

Printers have their own vocabulary, which can best be regarded as an occupational dialect. An *em quad* is a space as wide as the type size it belongs to is deep, and an *en quad* is half this width. The names are given because the letters 'm' and 'n' are cast on bodies of approximately these widths. In a busy and noisy composing room the words 'em' and 'en' are very liable to be confused with each other, and printers therefore call these spaces *muttons* and *nuts* respectively. A desire to avoid ambiguity explains the printer's use of *lower-case* to denote letters which are not capitals. In the days of hand-typesetting the capital letters were in the upper of two cases (or trays) and the small letters in the lower case. A layman might describe such letters as *small*, but this term might be taken to denote small capitals. One piece of printers' slang is the name of the case set aside for the reception of defective type, which is useful only as scrap metal. This is known as the *hell box*, because it is where the bad type goes.[16] The technical language of printers has made one contribution to our everyday language, though its origin is unknown to many of those who use it. A compositor, when composing type by hand, has to read it backwards and the letters 'p' and 'q' are easily confused. An apprentice, learning to read type, therefore has to mind his p's and q's.

Early stages in the history of medicine have left their mark on the language. Many words rest on assumptions that have become obsolete, such as the doctrine of the four humours. Medieval physiologists thought that there were four liquids in the human body: blood, phlegm, bile and black bile. The first three of these do in fact exist, but the fourth is imaginary. Good health was thought to depend on the maintenance of a proper balance of these four humours. This balance was a man's *temperament* or *complexion*. A man with too much of any one humour was *sanguine*, *phlegmatic*, *bilious* or *melancholy*. Disturbance of the balance led to *distemper*, which was a variation from the proper mixture. Good or bad balance of the humours made a man *good-humoured* or *in a bad humour* respectively. *Complexion* acquired its present meaning from the belief that a good or bad balance of humours could be detected from the colour and appearance of the face. The words dealing with humours have been specialised in various ways. *Distemper* is now used chiefly of dogs, and *temper* generally means bad temper. An excess of one humour might lead to eccentricity, and an old meaning of *humorous* was 'eccentric'.

Besides the humours, which were liquid, the body was thought to contain volatile and aeriform substances called spirits, which fall into three groups: the natural, the vital and the animal. Hence we have such words and phrases as *high-spirited*, *a spirited horse*, *in low spirits* and *animal spirits*.

Many names of diseases are recorded from the sixteenth century, such as *catarrh*, *epilepsy*, *mumps* and *scurvy*. From the seventeenth century we have *goitre*, *pneumonia* and *rabies*. More recently we have many words which have become familiar in spite of their learned origin, such as *acidosis*, *anaemia*, *anaesthetic*, *bronchitis*, *coronary* and *diphtheria*. We often meet with words like *metabolism* and *entropy*, though our knowledge of their meaning may not be precise, and we know enough about dietetics to speak respectfully of *proteins* and disparagingly of *carbohydrates*.

Legal language has a number of easily recognisable characteristics. Sentences are long; an entire document may consist of a single sentence. Adjectives are rare and vague adverbs like *very* and *rather* are completely absent. It was the invention of a cartoonist that a jury found that the accused was very, very guilty. Compounds of an adverb with a preposition are common, as in *hereunto*, *hereunder* and *thereof*. Pairs or groups of near-synonyms are co-ordinated, as in 'breaking and entering', 'goods and chattels', and 'terms and conditions'. They are used to avoid uncertainty. In the words of Crystal and Davy: 'there developed a tendency to write in each alternative and rely on inclusiveness as a compensation for lack of precision.'[17]

When legal terms are used by laymen, it is natural that they should not have the precision of meaning that they have when used by lawyers, but it is important that they should not be used in a completely different sense, and lawyers must be allowed to say what the precise meaning is. It is therefore necessary to pay special attention to words whose legal sense is completely different from that which the layman might give to them by the use of common sense alone. Such a difference can arise from the application of the principle *ejusdem generis* 'of the same kind or nature'. This has been defined as:

> The rule that where particular words are followed by general words, the general words are limited to the same kind as the particular words. Thus, the Sunday Observance Act, 1677, s. 1, provides that 'no tradesman, artificer, workman, labourer, or other person whatsoever shall do or exercise any worldly labour, business or work of their

> ordinary callings upon the Lord's Day (works of necessity and charity only excepted)'. The words 'or other person whatsoever' are to be construed *ejusdem generis* with those which precede them so that an estate agent is not within the section.[18]

Without this ruling a layman might be excused for thinking that, if the word *whatsoever* has any meaning at all in this context, its purpose would be not to exclude anybody. Another principle is that if a list of specific words is not followed by a general term, all other things are implicitly excluded.

Legal English shows a high proportion of French and Latin loan-words. Some technical terms in Law French or Law Latin are part of the legal vocabulary; examples are French *entail*, *mortgage* and *tort* and Latin *subpoena*, *affidavit* and *habeas corpus*. A number of words that were once thought of as legal terms have passed into our everyday language; examples are *rent*, *attach*, *purchase*, *claim*, *culprit*, *assets* and *divorce*. Such words can puzzle the layman. Many of us, when filling up forms, have had no difficulty about giving our address but have then been puzzled by a request for our domicile, since we thought that that was what 'address' meant. Our difficulties would have been lessened if the form had asked for our 'permanent residence'.

Some technical terms, in losing their legal sense, have undergone changes which must be regarded as unfortunate, since the terms once had a useful precise meaning but have now acquired meanings for which we have plenty of words already. Such a word is *alibi*, whose legal meaning is a defence on the quite precise grounds that the accused was somewhere else at the time of the offence, but it has been extended to mean an excuse of any kind. Tony Weller's sorrowful comment on Mr Pickwick's lack of success in the trial of Bardell against Pickwick was 'Oh, Sammy, Sammy, vy worn't there a alleybi' (*Pickwick Papers*, ch. 34). *Hotch potch* is still in use as a legal term to denote the reunion and blending of properties for the purpose of securing equal division, especially when one is dealing with the property of an intestate parent, but it is most often used to denote a dish of many mixed ingredients, like mutton broth, or a mixture in general. *Paraphernalia* as a legal term denotes the articles of personal property which the law allows a married woman to regard as her own, but it is often used more generally to denote miscellaneous personal belongings regardless of ownership.

One can see the effect of a technical vocabulary in the language of diplomacy, the purpose of which is to secure what Lord Strang calls 'accommodations or agreements'. He says that the most likely way of achieving agreement is by 'seeking precision, by cultivating rationality rather than emotion, by practising guarded understatement, by avoiding irony, by taking the heat out of controversy, by inspiring confidence'. For this purpose 'they can draw upon a simple well-tried and internationally accepted diplomatic vocabulary – words like *détente* or *modus vivendi* – borrowed chiefly from Latin or French. They are also assisted by those mild diplomatic phrases by which governments can, by careful gradation of emphasis, say the plainest things to each other without raising their voices. They "cannot remain indifferent" to this. They view something "with grave concern". They may go further and say that they "will be obliged to consider their own interests", or – and this is a pretty serious thing to say – that they "decline to be responsible for the consequences".'[19]

Slang is plentiful in English literature from the sixteenth century onwards. It is most at home in the spoken language, and there can be little doubt that it was used in speech in earlier centuries but, since it has always been regarded as informal and not quite respectable, it has never had a very good chance of being preserved in literature. Its chief characteristic is novelty; the creator of slang is trying to get away from what he regards as outworn conventions. Slang is unsuited to formal use, though much depends on the personal preference of the speaker. The man who uses slang, like the retailer of obscenities, is making advances to his hearers, which they may resent because they don't like him and don't want to accept him as a member of a group who would quite happily use slang among themselves.

The result of the quest for novelty is that slang rarely has a long life. If a slang word achieves popularity, it becomes a convention as rigid as that against which it rebels. Few speakers are so conventional as habitual users, as distinct from inventors, of slang. They are eager to seize the inventions of others and to give them wider currency until the new words die from excessive use. In Philip Howard's expressive phrase, they 'soon become anachronistic and a laughing-stock, and die of embarrassment'.[20] If they do not pass out of use, they are accepted as standard; the words survive, but they cease to be slang.

The vocabulary of slang is constantly being renewed from that of the underworld. Our knowledge of such language as used in the past is for the most part not derived from those who used it as a natural form of speech, since such men were not much given to writing. It is derived rather from the work of pamphleteers of the time who collected such words for the amusement of their readers. Such pamphleteers were particularly active during the sixteenth century. Just as the Cockney rhyming slang of today is imitated by members of all social classes, the thieves' slang of the sixteenth century was collected in such works as Robert Greene's *Conny Catching* pamphlets (1591–2). A few of these words have survived in standard English, often with a change of meaning; examples are *prig*, *filch*, *munch* and *queer*. Others, such as *ken* 'house' and *hook* 'steal', have passed out of use; a few, like *grub* 'food' and *booze* 'drink', have remained in the language as slang.

Users of slang are ready to take words from any source, including dialect. To determine whether a word is dialect or slang we have to look at the linguistic and social background of the speaker. If a countryman complains of the *rheumatiz*, he may be using a dialectal form that comes naturally to him, but if a young man who is obviously not a dialect speaker uses the word, the chances are that it is a loan-word from dialect into slang, and it is sometimes possible to detect the quotation-marks in the speaker's voice.

Two conflicting tendencies are at work in the creation of slang: curtailment and exuberance. *Professor* becomes *prof*, and *mathematics* becomes *maths* in England and *math* in America, but some slang words, such as *absquatulate* and *ninctobinkus*, owe their popularity to their length and to the accidental resemblance of parts of them to other words of known meaning. Sometimes both tendencies are at work in the same word. *OK*, whatever its origin, owes much of its popularity to its brevity, which is carried a stage further in *oke*. Beyond this, curtailment can go no further without interfering with intelligibility and, since the user of slang cannot leave well alone, exuberance sets in and we get *okey-doke*.

Rhyming slang can easily become tiresome, and those who indulge in it have to seek for ways to relieve its dullness. One way is to omit the rhyming word from a phrase, thus exercising the hearer's ingenuity or his memory to supply the missing word. There can be many stages between the word intended and the one used, and devotees of rhyming slang show much ingenuity in preventing the meaning of a word from being immediately obvious. Thus an *Oxford* can be understood to mean twenty-five pence if we remember that it is a curtailment of *Oxford scholar* and that a dollar was at one time worth about five shillings. A hat can be called a *titfer* if we remember that this is a curtailment of *tit for tat*. Another way of relieving the tedium of rhyming slang is to choose a rhyming word that has some connexion in meaning with the word that it replaces. The connexion is usually cynical and based on the conventions of the comic picture postcard that marriages are unhappy and children tiresome. Thus we have *trouble and strife* for 'wife', *God forbids* for 'kids' and *artful dodger* for 'lodger'.

Back slang consists of familiar words disguised by being spelt backwards. Some words have passed from back slang into general slang without users being aware of their origin. Thus *boy* becomes *yob*, *penny* becomes *yennep* and *police* becomes *slop*.

When slang words pass into the standard language, their original sense may be lost and they may then be replaced by other words whose meaning is clear. *Pluck* originally meant the liver and lungs of an animal. It came to mean 'stamina' and then 'courage', and in this sense it is now a rather literary word, perhaps with special associations with stories for boys. Its place has been taken by *guts*, which has had a similar semantic development without so far achieving the respectability of *pluck*.

Several words have been borrowed from American slang,

such as *jazz*, *cagey* 'cautious', and *blurb*, a useful word to denote the advertisement on the wrapper of a book giving some idea of what the book is about. What else could you call it? A more recent borrowing is *gimmick*, originally meaning a device used by a conjuror in performing a trick, but the word has acquired a useful pejorative meaning when applied to someone who takes short cuts to achieve his dubious ends. *Scrounge* is one of many words, like *pinch* and *half-inch*, meaning 'to steal' but used in an attempt to persuade the hearer that the theft is not a blameworthy act. There is a similar attempt to gain sympathy in the use of the verb *wangle* 'to achieve something by improper contriving'. *Gadget* 'small and useful piece of mechanism' is first recorded as sailors' slang in the nineteenth century.

Abusive names for the inhabitants of particular countries are often slang. *Yankee* is probably from Dutch *Janke*, a diminutive of the name *Jan* used derisively; its original meaning was 'New Englander', but it is often applied to any inhabitant of the United States. *Dago* is from Spanish *Diego*, but it is often applied to an Italian. *Sawney*, a variant of *Sandy* and *Alexander*, is used as a derogatory term for a Scotsman. The frame of mind which leads to the coining of such names is sometimes called *Jingoism*. *Jingo*, as a term for a man who would today be called a *hawk* and contrasted with a *dove*, dates from 1878, when it was used in the refrain of a political song written in support of Disraeli's policy during the Russo-Turkish War.

Other terms of abuse have had a variety of origins. *Blackguard*, like *villain*, is a social term that has acquired a moral sense; it was used in the sixteenth and seventeenth centuries for a low-ranking servant in a large household, like *scullion*. *Blackleg* was slang for a swindler at race-meetings in the eighteenth century. *Bully* was a term of endearment in Shakespeare, but its meaning has changed for the worse. *Coxcomb* was originally the cap worn by a jester, but it has come to mean a conceited, showy person. *Fop* and *sot* once meant 'fool', but they have been specialised to denote different kinds of folly. *Chum* originally meant 'chamber-fellow'; its associations today are with old-fashioned stories for boys which use the language of the *Boy's Own Paper*. *Bombast* is from a Greek word meaning 'cotton wadding' borrowed through Latin and French; its application to an inflated style of speech or writing dates from the sixteenth century. *Fustian* has a similar meaning and history.

Slang follows the same patterns as the standard language, but the motives for its use are different. There is a constant straining after originality and humour in slang, which delights in violent and ludicrous metaphors, obscure analogies and meaningless words. Slang has its vogue-words. Indeed, fashion and novelty play such a prominent part in its creation that it may be said to consist entirely of vogue-words. A phrase currently in frequent use is 'down to the nitty-gritty', and this may be regarded as still slang, but 'the grass roots' has passed into idiom. The existence of one slang word can lead to the creation of another, which may not have such a secure place in the language. We have learnt to accept *debunk* as a useful word meaning to expose the falseness of a reputation, but we are less familiar with *rebunk* to denote the process of reaction which sets in when debunking has gone far enough. The subsequent fate of slang words is hard to foretell and we cannot be sure that *rebunk* will be generally accepted.

Many of the objections that are made to the use of slang could be made to the same tendencies when they operate in standard English. It is wasteful to pile up synonyms for 'good' and 'bad', as slang does, but the standard language shows the same tendency. In its quest for novelty slang adds to the number of unnecessary synonyms, but a language has its own way of dealing with the problem: when then the newly created synonyms cease to be novel, they generally pass out of use, but if the new words serve a real need, they are adopted into the standard language.

Slang includes many coinages and distortions of existing words, and the etymology of many slang words is unknown. What, for example, is the origin of *banter* or *bamboozle*? *Sham* may be a northern dialect pronunciation of *shame*. *Doggerel* is first found in *The Canterbury Tales*, where the Host protests against the 'rym dogerel' of the tale of Sir Thopas; the etymology is unknown but the meaning of the word may have been influenced by such words as *dog-Latin*. Some words which have at one time been slang are from foreign phrases, like *carouse* from German *gar aus (trinken)*, *hoax* from Latin *hocus (pocus)* and *factotum* from Latin *fac*, the imperative of *facere*, and *totum*, the neuter of *totus*. Students may well have played a part in the creation of such words.

Many words and phrases which are today accepted as normal standard English were condemned as slang when they were first used. These include *downfall*, *man-of-war*, *nowadays*, *wherewithal*, *workmanship*, and phrases like 'to drive a bargain' and 'to handle a subject'. Some words that begin as slang go to the other extreme and remain in the language as excessively literary words, such as *purport* and *encroach*.

CHAPTER FIVE

Semantics

Semantics is the branch of the study of language which deals with the meanings of words. In public discussions, on the radio and elsewhere, it is a common practice for one of the disputants to dismiss his opponent's argument by saying that it is merely a matter of semantics, while he goes on to reiterate his own arguments. This approach is open to two objections. The first is the use of the word 'merely'. When disputants are arguing with words – and no other method of argument is in general use – the meanings that they attach to the words they use are of fundamental importance, not something to be dismissed. The second objection is that the comment should be followed, as it rarely is, by an examination of what semantic problems are involved and how they affect the argument.

One indication of the value of any subject of study is the extent to which it enables us to link up isolated scraps of information into a whole, and the study of semantics often helps us to make such a link. The development of meaning of one word may throw light on that of another. Even if the two words are of quite different origin and meaning, it is possible to see the same tendencies, such as specialisation or elevation of meaning, at work, and any suggested explanation of form or meaning gains in credibility if a parallel can be quoted.

A knowledge of the history of words is necessary if we are to read an author who wrote some centuries ago with any hope of finding out what he intended, as distinct from the effect which his words may accidentally produce on a modern reader. The various kinds of semantic development have been illustrated by several comparisons. One kind has been described as ramification. A word acquires new meanings as a tree throws out new branches, but the new branches do not necessarily kill the old, though they may overshadow them. In a few quite common words an old meaning has been completely lost. For example, *cloud* is from OE *clūd*, which meant a mass of rock or earth. The word was used metaphorically to denote a mass of visible condensed watery vapour in the sky, and the metaphorical sense has completely replaced the original meaning. *Cloud* has thus taken over many of the meanings of OE *wolcen* which, as *welkin*, has remained only in poetic and literary use.

Most words have several different meanings, but this variety causes no trouble to the average speaker of a language, because the context usually makes it clear which meaning is intended. A word may be deliberately understood in a sense not intended by the speaker, as in the exchange between a judge and a barrister who had dealt at some length with a legal point. The judge was unimpressed and said testily 'I'm no wiser'. The barrister replied urbanely 'No, my lord, but much better informed'. We learn to accept quite surprising changes of meaning, and only a speaker very unfamiliar with English is tempted to reply to an invitation to have a dry sherry by saying 'Don't be silly'. We may suffer a temporary shock on hearing that a man married a typewriter or that a girl married an Alsatian, but a little research shows that *typewriter* was often used in the nineteenth century with the meaning 'typist' and that *Alsatian* is a proper term for a man who comes from Alsace. An extension in the range of meanings of a common word can throw an interesting light on the mental processes of the speaker, as when an American said indignantly 'To charge twenty-five cents for a slice of apple pie just isn't democratic'. It can also illustrate differences in the approach to a subject, as when a member of an Oxford debating team visiting America was puzzled by the congratulations that he received on a speech: 'You certainly are a credit to your department of phonetics'.

Words of similar meaning fall into groups, and a change in the meaning of one word in the group can cause another word to slip into the place of the word that has changed. The original meaning of *slay* (OE *slēan*) was 'to strike'. When this verb took over the stronger meaning of its compound *ofslēan* 'to kill', its original meaning was expressed by verbs such as *strike* (OE *strīcan* 'to go, stroke'), *smite* (OE *smītan* 'to smear') and *hit* (ON *hitta* 'to meet with').

Association with other words sometimes leads to misunderstanding. C. S. Lewis illustrates this danger:

> A word needs to be very careful about the phonetic company it keeps. The old meaning of *obnoxious* has been almost destroyed by the combined influence of *objectionable* and *noxious*, and that of *deprecate* by *depreciate* and that of *turgid* by *turbid*.[1]

Any reader can provide further examples from his own experience. In the minds of many speakers the meaning of *flout* has been influenced by *flaunt*, *scarify* by *scare* and *sternum* by the noun *stern*.

Some words change their meanings as a result of frequent use in particular phrases, which results in specialisation of meaning. Thus 'the enormity of the offence' spoils *enormity* for use in a colourless or laudatory sense. *Chunk*, *chore* and *gang* are frequently used by low-brows or, even more often, by speakers trying to enlist low-brow sympathies. Hence they are not suited to contexts involving intellectual discussion. *Condign* in Shakespeare meant 'worthily deserved', as in 'condign praise' (*Love's Labour's Lost*, I.2.27), but it has acquired derogatory associations through frequent use in the phrase 'condign punishment'. In the sixteenth century *companion* underwent a similar fate through use with words like 'base', but it has now lost its pejorative sense.

There is room for argument whether a word ever has a 'true' meaning; for practical purposes we assume that the true meaning of a word is that given to it in a particular context by most of the people with whom we come into contact. There is a similar uncertainty about how far it is proper to speak of a mistake in the use of a word. If one speaker uses a word in an unusual sense, he is liable to be accused of making a mistake; if a number of other speakers follow his example, they add a new meaning to those that the word already possesses. Semantic change begins with such 'mistakes'.

Negative statements about the meaning of a word may have a value that their speakers do not intend them to have.

The fact that the speaker thinks a denial necessary is evidence that the word is sometimes used in that sense.

Words denoting rank have tended to change so as to denote character or behaviour appropriate to that rank. In consequence words denoting high rank become terms of praise whereas those denoting low rank become terms of disapproval. Examples are *chivalrous*, *courteous*, *frank*, *generous*, *liberal* and *noble* beside *churlish*, *ignoble*, *villainous* and *vulgar*. Similarly nouns denoting the victims of misfortune have come to express blame as well as pity. *Wretch* (OE *wrecca* 'exile') is used to express both pity and contempt, and the archaic *caitiff* (ultimately from Latin *captivus*) is chiefly used as a term of abuse.

There are two important ways in which meaning can develop, known respectively as radiation and concatenation. When radiation takes place, the new meanings are derived independently from the original meaning. The various senses of *head* are mostly derived from its meaning 'part of the body'. Concatenation, a derivative of Latin *catena* 'chain', is the development by which a second meaning derives naturally from the first, a third from the second, and so on, with the result that the final meaning of the word may differ completely from the original sense. At first the older meanings remain in use side by side with the new, but they are often lost and the new meanings can begin their own processes of change, which may be by radiation or concatenation or both. In medieval times an *escheat* was the lapsing of property to the government or the lord of the manor when a man died without heirs, and the officer who looked after such confiscation was known as an *escheater*, later a *cheater*. Naturally such officers were unpopular and fraud was not unknown, with the result that *cheat* came to be used to denote fraud of any kind. An example of the differences which concatenation can produce between the original and later meanings of a word is provided by *treacle*, which is derived from a Greek word meaning 'pertaining to a wild animal' but which now means 'a sweet syrup'. The stages are: a remedy for the bite of a wild animal, a remedy in the form of a syrup and a syrup not necessarily remedial.

By figurative usage words originally denoting concrete objects have come to express abstract ideas. *Long* and *short* originally referred to dimensions in space, but they have been transferred to denote extension in time. The origin of *balderdash* is unknown, but in the seventeenth century it meant a frothy mixture of drinks; it has now acquired the abstract meaning of nonsense, spoken or written. *Ruminate* originally referred to an animal chewing its cud; later, by a pleasing metaphor, it referred to thought. Other words which today have a similar meaning have had a wide variety of origins, all illustrating the movement from concrete to abstract. *Ponder* meant 'to weigh'; *reflect* is from Latin *reflectere* 'to bend back'; *calculate* is from Latin *calculus* 'pebble' and *investigate* from Latin *vestigium* 'footprint'. Movement in the opposite direction, from abstract to concrete, is sometimes found. *Anatomy* 'the science of bodily structure' is sometimes used jocularly with the meaning 'body'.

Words can have such a wide range of meanings that they acquire a precise sense only in a particular context. English has many words which, like Latin *res*, can refer to almost anything; such words are *thing*, *matter*, *affair*, *circumstance* and *condition*. Most of these words once had a more precise meaning. For example, *thing* originally meant a legislative or judicial assembly.

A change in meaning may take the form of a transferred epithet. An adjective is transferred from a person or thing possessing a particular quality to another where it is not strictly appropriate. Such transfers are especially common in poetry; examples in non-literary use are 'joyful news' and 'hopeless efforts'. *Curious* is from Latin *curiosus* 'taking care'. When it means 'inquisitive' it is still applied to a person, but when it means 'peculiar' it is generally applied to a person or thing in the sense 'requiring care'. *Secure* is from Latin *securus* 'without anxiety' and it is still applied to persons with that sense, but it is now more often applied to objects that are so carefully guarded that their owners have no need to worry; a similar meaning has been acquired by its derivative *securities*. Transference from things to persons is less common; examples are the adjectives *straightforward* and *pompous* when applied to human beings. Other examples of transference are *disaster*, originally meaning the unfavourable aspect of a star, which has come to mean a calamity, and *polite*, originally meaning 'polished' but now applied metaphorically to both utterances and those who utter them. *Game* originally meant 'sport'; it was specialised to mean 'hunting' and then transferred to the birds that are killed. In much the same way *venison* meant first 'hunting' and then 'the flesh of the deer'.

Transitive verbs may become intransitive and intransitive verbs may become causative, as when we speak of flying a kite. The older method of forming a causative, by the use of a different suffix which, after various sound-changes, has given us *lay* beside *lie* and *set* beside *sit*, has been found to be unnecessary.

One result of semantic change is an increase in the number of near-synonyms in the language, since we may already have a word to express the meaning that a new word may acquire. Words can be regarded as exact synonyms only if they are completely interchangeable in all contexts. The difference between a native word and a loan-word of similar meaning may be that one word expresses approval or is neutral while the other expresses disapproval, as in *boyish* and *puerile*. There may be emotional differences: a man who is *lonely* is more unhappy than one who is merely *solitary*, and relations that are *friendly* are more pleasant than those that are *amicable*. Anyone may sit on a *stool* but only a king or a queen should sit on a *throne*, just as anyone may live in a *house* but only a rich man can afford to live in a *mansion*. We may notice similar differences between *brotherly* and *fraternal*, *hearty* and *cordial*, and *heavenly* and *celestial*. As a result of the borrowing of Latinised adjectives and their use side by side with native nouns, there is often no connexion in form between nouns and the corresponding adjectives, so that we get *eye* and *ocular*, *mouth* and *oral*, *moon* and *lunar*, and *son* and *filial*. The richness of our vocabulary is increased by the existence of several different suffixes to form adjectives from nouns, each giving a slightly different shade of meaning. Thus we have *earthen*, *earthly* and *earthy*, all expressing different meanings.

A common form of semantic development is specialisation of meaning, which provides a use for words which might otherwise become obsolete. When, as a result of borrowing from another language, we find two words denoting the same idea, it is a natural development for one of them to remain general while the other comes to denote some subdivision of the general class. In Old English, *gān* and *wadan* both meant 'to move forward'; *go* remained general while *wade* came to mean 'to move forward through water'. Another example of specialisation is *grocer*, which originally meant 'wholesaler' (OFr *grossier*). Among the things he sells are *spices*, which have undergone a similar development. *Spice* (OFr *espice*) is a doublet of *species* (Latin *species* 'kind, variety'). A similar development is seen in the use of *deal* to denote any kind of cheap wood. There is no such thing as a deal tree, but *deal* (OE *dǣl* 'part') came to be used to denote a quantity of wood of quality so undistinguished that there was no point in specifying what kind of tree it came from. *Garment*, *shroud* and *weed* were once near-synonyms. *Shroud* acquired the sense 'winding sheet' in the second half of the sixteenth century, *weed* was restricted to a widow's mourning garment at about the same time, and *garment* has remained general. Other examples of specialisation are *deer*, which once meant 'animal', and *fowl*, which once meant 'bird'. OE *steorfan* 'to die' has given *starve*, which in standard English means 'to die from hunger', whereas in dialects it means 'to die (or suffer) from cold' – two different examples of specialisation.

Some words undergo different kinds of semantic development at different periods of their history. *Nice* is ultimately from Latin *nescius* 'ignorant'. It came to mean 'fastidious' and we still speak of making nice distinctions. In the eighteenth century it became a vogue-word as an all-purpose term of praise, and its use in this sense is satirised in chapter 14 of *Northanger Abbey*.

The wide variety of nouns denoting groups of animals goes back to a time before Englishmen had become familiar with the practice of classification; they spoke of a *herd* of cattle, a *pride* of lions, a *swarm* of bees and a *covey* of partridge because they were not familiar with the abstract idea of a group. Many such group-names are recorded in the fifteenth-century *Book of Saint Albans* and they have been kept living or partly living by antiquarian interest in their variety. There have been some modern attempts to add to their number, but these have been jokes rather than serious attempts to enrich the language; they have produced such nonce-usages as 'a loiter of lecturers' and 'an absence of professors'. There is a similar variety of different words to denote the places where animals are kept. Horses, cows, dogs, pigs and rabbits are kept respectively in stables, byres, kennels, sties and hutches. Such variety is often mentioned with implied pride when we speak of the richness of the English vocabulary, but it makes the language needlessly difficult to learn.

When a word becomes restricted in meaning, its earlier and more general meaning is generally taken over by another word. Thus OE *fugol* meant 'bird', but when the meaning of *fowl* was restricted to that of a large farmyard bird suitable for eating, the more general sense was taken over by *bird* (OE *bridd*), which originally meant 'young bird'. This change involved extension of meaning in the new word, and the extension can be paralleled in both English and other languages. *Rabbit*, which originally meant 'young rabbit', has replaced *cony*, and in French *oiseau* was originally a diminutive 'young bird'. These two processes of extension and restriction have been especially common in English, because our readiness to adopt loan-words has supplied us with a good stock of words to use as replacements.

Specialisation of meaning often results from the omission of an adjective or other defining word. An *undertaker* is a funeral undertaker; a *glass* is a drinking glass, and a *paper* is a newspaper. The defining word may never have been used, although it is always understood, and the restriction may be too vague to express in a single word. Context of situation usually indicates what restriction is intended. To an actor, as to most members of the general public, a theatre is a place where plays are performed, but to a hospital nurse it is an operating theatre. On the other hand, specialisation may result from the omission of a noun while an adjective remains. A *private* is a private soldier and a *general* is a general officer. An *editorial* is an editorial article and a *lyric* is a lyric poem, originally one composed for the lyre.

Change of meaning from abstract to concrete usually involves specialisation. *Provision* is an abstract noun denoting the act of seeing into the future, but it soon came to denote the action taken as a result of such vision, and it is now commonly used in the plural to denote goods bought for consumption. We can use the abstract noun *majesty* in addressing the sovereign, and a man may be described variously as a *success*, a *failure* or a *fraud*.

A word may be transferred from one specialised sense to another. An abstract meaning, later lost, may be the link between the two meanings. A *dreadnought* was originally a thick coat or waterproof; clad in it one had no need to fear the rain. The word was later applied to a new type of battleship, launched in 1906, which was superior in armament to all its predecessors; in such a ship one had no need to fear an enemy's attack.

A few of the large number of examples of specialisation may be given. *Affection* meant 'feeling' in Elizabethan English. *Asphyxia*, from the Greek word for 'pulse', originally meant the cessation of pulsation from any cause, not merely from suffocation. *Ballade* has been specialised further than its doublet *ballad*; each stanza of a ballade ends with a refrain and there is an envoi. *Disease* once meant any sort of discomfort, not necessarily illness. *Fond* is from the past participle of a verb meaning 'to be foolish'; it was specialised to refer to a doting affection and then lost its pejorative sense. *Goods* originally meant good things, not merely possessions. *Liquid*, *liquor* and *liqueur* are from the same root, but *liquid* has kept its wider sense while the other two words have been specialised. *Meat* was once food of any kind; it has kept its older sense in *sweetmeat* and the proverb 'One man's meat is another man's poison'. *Pocket* once meant 'little bag'; it is a diminutive of the Shakespearean *poke*, out of which Touchstone took a dial (*As You Like It*, II.7.20). *Poet* is ultimately from a Greek word meaning 'maker', and *maker* is used in the sense 'poet' in Elizabethan English. *Spill* originally meant 'destroy' but the meaning has been weakened; in Anglo-Saxon times you could spill your enemies whereas today we spill the milk. *Tyrant* is from a Greek word meaning an absolute ruler, not necessarily an oppressive one.

Types of semantic change tend to run in pairs, and side by side with specialisation we find generalisation, where the sense of a word becomes wider. Names of parts of the body are often extended, as when we speak of the head of a school, the foot of a page or a chest of drawers. There has been a constant search for a term to denote a human being in the widest sense. *Wight* is now archaic and *body* is used chiefly in compounds like *somebody* or *anybody*. *Person*, borrowed through French from Latin *persona* 'actor's mask', can apply to either sex; other terms which apply especially to men and which are colloquial or slang include *chap*, shortened from *chapman* 'pedlar', *merchant*, *character* and *fellow* (ON *félagi* 'business partner'). Words of several different origins have come to mean 'become'. *Become* itself is made up of *come* and a prefix and once meant 'arrive'. The usual Old English word was *weorðan*, which survives, if you can call it surviving, in the poetical phrase 'Woe worth the day!' Other words are illustrated in the sentences 'he turned pale', 'he went white' and 'it's growing cold'. There was no doubt similar generalisation in the very distant past to allow the falling together of quite different verbs to give the various parts of the verb 'to be': *be*, *is*, *am* and *was*.

Some words which now have similar meanings once had widely different meanings that have been generalised. A *necromancer* called up the spirits of the dead; a *wizard* was 'a wise man'; a *soothsayer* was 'a truthteller', and an *enchanter* was one who sang chants or charms. A *town* was an enclosure, an apt description of the stockaded settlements of the Germanic peoples; *city* is an abstract term from French *cité*, from Latin *civitas*, which originally meant 'citizenship', but it came to mean 'citizens' and then the place where they lived; *village* is borrowed through French from Latin *villaticus* 'belonging to a country house'; *hamlet* is a double diminutive of the word that has given *home*.

There is a widespread tendency for words denoting concrete objects or physical actions to extend their meaning to cover a number of figurative senses, and sometimes the original literal sense is lost, leaving only the metaphor. *Thrill* (OE *þyrelian*) is related to *through* and originally meant 'to pierce', but the literal sense has now been lost.

Some further examples of generalisation may be given. *Assassin* is from an Arabic word meaning 'hashish-eater'. The name was given to Muslim fanatics at the time of the Crusades who were sent on murder missions when intoxicated with hashish. A *costermonger* was a man who sold costard apples. A *layman* was originally a man not in holy orders and this is still its most common meaning, but the word is often used to mean a non-member of other professions, the particular profession being indicated by the context. *Paper* was originally a substitute for parchment made from the papyrus plant. It is now made from many different materials, including rags and wood pulp. A *scene* was originally the tent in front of which a Greek play was performed; it then became a permanent part of a Greek theatre, forming the background of the stage. It is now often used in non-dramatic senses to denote the place where something is happening, as in 'the scene of the crime'.

A tendency that explains many changes of meaning is that known as degeneration or pejorative sense-development. It is often a form of specialisation: a colourless or laudatory descriptive adjective is used so often with an innuendo that the innuendo becomes part of the meaning of the word. Thus *sanctimonious* in Shakespeare means 'holy', but when the word is used today there is always an implication that the holiness is only superficial. Other words that show pejorative development as a form of specialisation are *stink*, which originally had a neutral sense, *lust*, which in Old English meant 'pleasure', and *wench*, once a neutral term for a girl, later disrespectful and now generally jocular or dialectal.

Degeneration can result from faded euphemism or hyperbole, as in such words as *insane*, *insolent*, *terrific*, *vulgar*, *common* and *plain*. The determined optimism of school reports, which leads to the use of *fair* with the meaning of 'mediocre', has debased the meaning of *fair*. *Mean* originally meant 'middling', but it has come to mean something much worse than that, just as, in a world that thinks highly of youth, *middle-aged* is applied to someone well past the middle years of the average human life. *Questionable*, when applied to conduct, generally means 'unquestionably bad'. In order to avoid giving pain by saying that a student has done badly in an examination, the term *unclassified* is sometimes used.

Since faint praise is felt to be damning, some words of moderate praise, such as *worthy*, have come to be terms of rather patronising abuse. *Silly*, which originally meant 'blessed' or 'happy', has come to mean 'foolish' from a cynical assumption that no one would be happy if he had enough sense to know what was coming to him. Terms of praise that are felt to be pretentious become terms of abuse. *Egregious* and *ineffable*, *grandiose* and *grandiloquent* have developed in this way. *Specious* once meant 'beautiful', but it is now usually applied to an argument which at first seems sound but which will not stand up to examination. *Doughty* is from an Old English adjective meaning 'valiant'. It is still a term of praise, but it has often been used ironically and it is now generally used with a reservation that it refers to deeds that are very good if you like that sort of thing.

It would be rash to assume that country-dwellers are less intelligent that town-dwellers, but until recently it was widely assumed that people who live in the country are slow on the uptake and morally deficient. This attitude is reflected in several words which involve moral or intellectual disparagement. *Pagan* originally meant someone who lived on a heath and *villain* was a term for a serf whose work was mainly on a farm. *Boor* once meant a farmer; now it means a clumsy or ill-bred person. *Peasant*, from a French word meaning 'countryman', now denotes a man of low social class. *Rustic* is an emotive word, sometimes used admiringly, as when we speak of rustic simplicity, but more often disparagingly; the colourless adjective is *rural*. In contrast, *civil* and *urbane*, which originally described town-dwellers, are now terms of praise, though the praise is sometimes faint.

Words denoting domestic service have tended to degenerate. *Slavish* and *servile* are derogatory adjectives to describe those who acquiesce in their humble condition. *Maid* originally meant 'young woman'; it was specialised to denote a servant and it now tends to be avoided. Recent attempts to disguise the realities of domestic service, such as *domestic*, *domesticated person* or *cleaning lady*, have not undergone degeneration but their use reflects the widespread belief that it is something to be glossed over. Words denoting male servants have undergone more drastic degeneration. *Knave* originally meant 'boy' or 'servant' and *varlet*, a variant of *valet*, originally meant a knight's attendant; today, when it is used at all, it is a jocular or archaic term of abuse.

Greenough and Kittredge point out[2] that changes in meaning often began to take place before a word entered the

English language. In explaining loan-words we have to pay attention to the whole history of the word in question. The principles of semantic change are based upon habits of thought that are shared by human beings of many different nationalities, and it is easy to find foreign parallels to English semantic development that are not likely to be due to borrowing.

Degeneration can affect the dignity or standing of a word as well as its meaning. *Shove* is today a colloquial word that would not be used in a dignified context, but it is used in Old English heroic poetry. *Naughty* expressed strong condemnation in Old English; it has been weakened by its use to describe the misdemeanours of children and it is used by adults who are trying to make light of their own transgressions. *Twit* 'to reproach' is today used only of trivial wrongdoing, but in Old English it could be used when the charge was cowardice, the most heinous of offences. *Worthy* once meant 'honourable' but it has become condescending. The related word *worship* has none of these associations, but it has acquired a strengthened sense in religious use and a specialised legal sense in 'Your Worship'. *Respectable* has had a history similar to that of *worthy*. Changes in the status or meaning of words are not always shared by derivatives, and we can arrive at the original meaning of *respectable* by thinking of *respect*; its patronising use was well established in the nineteenth century.

A common form of degradation of status is that which makes a word unsuitable for poetic use. Chaucer's Manciple was more than a match for 'an heep of lerned men'. For Chaucer *heap* had not the commonplace associations that it has for us. In Elizabethan times the liver was as dignified as the heart, and it was thought of as the seat of courage; when we use the word today we tend to think of the butcher. Other words that have become undignified are *crack*, *spout* and the verbs *fry* and *wag*.

Some words have a low status because they deal with subjects that are thought to be unpleasant. They are generally short and are liable to be excluded from dictionaries, though a lot depends on the size of the dictionary and the policy of its editor. Dr Johnson made an often-quoted reply to a lady who congratulated him on having excluded improper words from his dictionary: 'You have evidently been looking for them, madam'. There is no clear-cut line of division between words which are tolerated and those which are not, and fashions change. George H. McKnight has shown what a large number of words which were frowned upon in the eighteenth century are now perfectly acceptable:

> Certain it is that the list of words raised in the course of the eighteenth century from low or obscure origin to reputable use is an impressive one. Among words branded at one time or another by eighteenth-century purists either as cant or as slang or as 'low' are: *banter*, *cocksure*, *dumbfound*, *doodle*, *enthusiasm*, *extra*, *flimsy*, *flippant*, *flirtation*, *fun*, *gambling*, *hanker*, *helter-skelter*, *humbug*, *jilt*, *kidney*, *mob*, *nervous*, *noodle*, *palming*, *pell-mell*, *prig*, *quandary*, *shabby*, *sham*, *shuffle*, *topsy-turvy*, *touchy*, *turtle*, *twang*.[3]

There is always a strong subjective element in the assessment of the status of words, but one is struck by the varying fortunes of these words in later English. Some, like *extra* and *nervous*, have become part of our normal vocabulary, suitable for use on all occasions, and most of the people who use them would be surprised to learn that they were ever frowned upon. Others, like *hanker* and *humbug*, are still colloquial though, like other colloquialisms, they are sometimes used on formal occasions by those who aim at a forceful style. The most interesting fate is that of words like *dumbfound* and *quandary*, which have undergone a complete change of status from the substandard to the formal and literary.

What we want to know about a word is whether it is the sort of word that an educated Englishman would not only understand but use without self-consciousness. Is it suitable for formal or informal use? We acquire such knowledge about our native language unconsciously, but foreigners have more difficulty. A dictionary will not answer such questions with precision and often there is no precise answer. Subtleties have to be left to the individual speaker; one can simply say that a given word is not the sort of word that would be used in a particular context or among a particular group of people. A German student living in England complained that he had found many pitfalls in the use of the language. When asked to give an example, he said that his partner at a dance had taken offence when he paid her what he thought was a graceful compliment. The compliment that had caused offence was 'You have a very nice body'. When asked how he knew that it was not a success, he replied 'She became red'.

Intensifying adverbs have followed one another in quick succession as each has passed out of fashion, weakened by over-use. OE *swīðe* became obsolete, to be replaced in Middle English by *full*. In the sixteenth century *passing* was common. *Very* has had a long life since Mercutio complained of its excessive use; people still complain of it today and, with even more justification, of its emphatic repetition *very very*. Another way of strengthening *very* is by the addition of *indeed*: 'Thank you very much indeed'. Slang has *awfully* and Scots has *awfu'*. More recent slang intensives are *mighty*, *real* and *dead*.

Words reflect the esteem in which the objects that they denote are held. At the time of the Renaissance medieval scholarship fell into disrepute, and some words associated with it acquired pejorative associations that they have never lost. Duns Scotus (d. 1308) was ridiculed by sixteenth-century humanists, and their low opinion is preserved in the meaning that we give to *dunce*. The medieval university course of grammar, logic and rhetoric was known as the *trivium*, and the belief that these subjects were unimportant has given the adjective *trivial* its modern meaning. In much the same way Greek *sophisma* 'clever device', a derivative of *sophos* 'wise', acquired a derogatory meaning which has been preserved in such words as *sophism*, *sophist* and *sophistry*. We are liable to distrust both too much and too little knowledge. *Cunning* 'having knowledge', *crafty* 'skilled in a craft' and *sly* (from ON *slœgr* 'skilful') have all become terms of disparagement, but so too have such words as *simple*, *guileless* and *innocent*, which were applied to people without special knowledge.

A large number of miscellaneous words show pejorative development. *Apathy* is from a Greek word meaning freedom from domination by the passions; it is now used disparagingly of a sluggish condition of the mind. *Asylum*, another loan from Greek, originally meant a place where one was free from risk of capture, hence 'place of refuge', but, since many insane persons were sent to an asylum without having any choice in the matter, it came to mean a place of confinement. *Counterfeit* at first meant a copy, without any sinister suggestion, as when Bassanio refers to 'fair Portia's counterfeit' in *The Merchant of Venice* (III.2.115). *Dapper* is cognate with German *tapfer* 'brave'; it is now applied to a man careful of his appearance but without warlike qualities. *Enthusiasm* originally meant 'inspiration'; in the eighteenth century it underwent a semantic dip to mean 'fanaticism', from which it has recovered, since the quality which it denotes is now held in higher esteem. *To garble* originally meant 'to sift'; it still implies selection, but now it means to select facts in such a way as to give a distorted impression. *Inquisitive*, like *curiosity*, has degenerated because it is assumed that the interest that we show is in something that is not our business. *Lewd* originally meant 'belonging to the laity'; it came to mean 'ignorant' and then 'lascivious'. *Plausible* is cognate with *applause* and originally meant 'deserving approval', but the meaning has been restricted to mean something which seems reasonable at first but is not completely convincing. *Sullen* is a doublet of *solemn* used by people who find solemnity unattractive. *Vile* is from Latin *vilis* 'cheap' but the meaning has been degraded to make it a term of strong abuse.

Elevation of meaning is less common than degeneration. We sometimes find divergent changes, with two words of similar meaning developing in opposite directions. *Childish* and *juvenile* have sunk; *child-like*, *boyish* and *youthful* have risen. *Service* is something that we are proud to render, but *servility* is a quality that we do not want to possess.

Elevation may be accompanied by restriction or extension. *Splendid* once meant 'bright' but it has joined the large number of vague words of praise, along with *magnificent*, originally 'making large', a word whose development reflects the belief that big is beautiful. *Distinguished* once meant 'differentiated' without the implication that the difference involved excellence. Similarly *fame* meant 'report' in general; by restriction it has come to mean 'favourable report'.

Words may rise in dignity by association with institutions held in high esteem. *Marshal* originally meant 'horse-servant' and *chamberlain* meant 'the servant in charge of the household' but, since both of these were in the royal service, their occupations became titles of honour. *Knight* has diverged in meaning from *knave*. In Old English both *cniht* and *cnafa* meant 'boy' or 'youth' and both were expected to give service, but the service of a knight was military and at a high level and the word has therefore been elevated in meaning. Other examples of elevation are *ambition*, which originally meant 'canvassing for votes', *barter* (AN *baratour* 'trickster') and *boudoir* (cf. Fr *bouder* 'to sulk').

Euphemism has played an important part in the development of meaning. We may avoid direct reference to an object for two quite different reasons: because we find it unpleasant or because we feel that it is too sacred to be mentioned in trivial conversation. Only the first of these motives leads to euphemism but, whatever the motive for avoidance, the result is the same. A general term that covers both motives is 'taboo'. Taboos are concerned with registers as well as with semantics, because they vary according to the social context in which a word is used. Words that would not be acceptable in mixed company can be used without offence in a small homogeneous group. Since the written word may be read by members of many different groups, we tend to be more rigorous in our attitude to taboos when we are writing than when we are speaking.

The reasons for using euphemisms are varied. There are certain subjects, like sex, death and drunkenness, that are productive of taboos, but they vary from age to age. We tend to fight shy of references to death, but Victorian novelists loved them. We have to distinguish between a subject and specific words referring to that subject. Many readers of novels are passionately interested in sex but, until recently, novelists avoided explicitness.

Euphemism is provoked by references to parts of the body, giving *tummy* for 'stomach' and *anatomy* for 'body', bodily functions, giving *perspire* and *expectorate*, death, which tends to be called *passing away*, and disease, especially when mental.

The word *disease* itself is a euphemism, since its literal meaning is 'discomfort', and *mad* is replaced by a number of less specific terms, like *deranged* or *insane* (literally 'unhealthy').

Some euphemisms arise from a desire not to seem intolerant of other people's opinions. Instead of calling a man an infidel or an atheist, we call him a freethinker. The etymological meaning of *immoral* is 'ill-mannered' (cf. Latin *mores*). *Impertinent* originally meant 'irrelevant' but its meaning has now been strengthened to 'impudent'. *Indolent* meant 'not grieving' and *insolent* meant 'not accustomed'.

Euphemism covers not only the avoidance of the unpleasant but the pretentious search for imposing words to express commonplace ideas. A barber may describe himself as a *hair stylist* or a *hair specialist*. The high prestige of the medical profession causes words with medical associations to be much used by laymen. After all, we all specialise and we are all consulted from time to time, so what is to prevent a man from calling himself a *kitchen conversion specialist* or an *insurance consultant*? In public relations a euphemistic phrase can convince the unwary victim of a raw deal that he is the recipient of a favour. When a series of repeated radio programmes is announced, it sounds much better if we are told that listeners will have another opportunity to hear it.

Profane language has given rise to a large number of distortions which resemble the original in sound but which, apart from this resemblance, have little meaning. Thus we have *gee whiz* for 'Jesus' and *goodness*, *gosh* and *golly*, all replacing 'God'. The influence of the written language is to be seen in expressions like *dash it* and *darn it*, which probably arose from attempts to pronounce *d—* and *d—n* respectively. The substituted word may be a curtailment or a diminutive, and the curtailment may be so drastic as to leave merely an inflexional ending, as in *zounds* and *'sdeath*. *Gad* was preserved as a replacement for *God* after the form with unrounded vowel had passed out of general use. Euphemisms may become features of class dialect, as can be seen by comparing two famous comments. Thomas Carlyle, at a public meeting where Margaret Fuller declared that she accepted the universe, is said to have growled 'By God, she'd better'. A husband, reproached by his wife for letting her give him the best years of her life, said 'Gow, were them your best?' The two oaths are not interchangeable.

Words may become taboo in certain contexts because they are inappropriate or liable to misconstruction. The description 'beautiful' would not now be applied to a man except satirically, though it could be used without satire until the nineteenth century. It was generally replaced by 'handsome' and that in its turn is giving way to such adjectives as 'personable' and 'clean-cut'.

Euphemism takes many different forms. One type is the use of an entirely different word, like *shift*, which originally meant 'a change of clothes', for 'smock' or *drawers* for 'underpants'. Another common device is the use of a French loan-word like *lingerie* 'underwear', *derrière* 'buttocks', *retroussé* 'snub', *décolleté* 'low-necked' and *déshabillé* 'not carefully dressed'. A word of Latin origin may be preferred to a native word. Many people, seeing portraits of George Eliot, must have been struck by the thought that she looked like a horse, but one critic toned down the comparison by referring to her 'nobly equine visage'. Some euphemisms are produced by the use of prefixes, as in *immorality*, *misconduct* and *misguided*, and others by the use of a long word for a short one, as in *dipsomaniac* 'sot', *effluvium* 'stench', *intoxicated* 'drunk', *perspiration* 'sweat', *underprivileged* 'poor' or *unmentionables* 'trousers'. In everyday use the learned word may be curtailed, as in *dipso*. A common device is the replacement of a word by the negative of its opposite, as in *disease* 'illness', *insane* 'mad', *unclean* 'dirty' and *untruth* 'lie'. Sometimes initials are used, as in *d.o.a.* 'dead on arrival', *g.b.h.* 'grievous bodily harm' and s.o.b. 'son of a bitch'.

Phrases, as well as single words, may be used euphemistically. In a law-abiding country every citizen is expected to help the police if required to do so, but when we read in a newspaper that a man is helping the police with their enquires, we tend to assume that he is in trouble. This is because the phrase has come to be used as a journalistic cliché to describe someone who is in the hands of the police but has not been charged with an offence.

Fashion plays a large part in the use of euphemisms. Euphemisms, like slang, depend for their effect on novelty and therefore they have a short life as euphemisms, though they may continue to be used in other senses. Sometimes the wheel comes full circle, and a tired euphemism may be replaced by a revived use of the plain descriptive term that it once displaced. The short life of euphemisms may be explained by remembering that many people who use them are really ashamed of doing so and will abandon a euphemism like *senior citizen* when its use arouses derision. *Undertaker*, originally a euphemism based on specialisation, is giving way to the more explicit *funeral director*. We are now more conscious of race than we used to be, and such consciousness leads to the use of euphemisms. *Nigger* was originally euphemistic but its use today causes serious offence while the simple *black* does not. The use of the phrase 'working like a nigger' in a newspaper provoked an angry letter of protest from a total stranger in St Lucia demanding an apology. The changing fortunes of euphemisms for 'black' have been traced by Philip Howard:

> The revolving cycle of euphemism has turned full circle in the United States: black has become acceptable, replacing Afro-American, which replaced Negro, which replaced coloured, which replaced darky, which in turn replaced black. Coloured is a flabby euphemism, and is considered contemptuous by those so described.
>
> The latest silly extremity into which we have been forced by euphemism is 'non-white', as if the rude Anglo-Saxon natives were ever remotely white, instead of a muddy beige and pink.[4]

It is a welcome sign that as a rule we like to be kind to one another that euphemism is more common than dysphemism, the use of a derogatory word in place of a pleasant one, but euphemism can provoke satirical comments designed to destroy its effectiveness. *Progressive* is generally used as a term of praise, like *positive* and *creative*, but it is useful to be reminded that these words are not terms of praise in themselves but only when applied to a praiseworthy activity. Such a reminder was given by the man who said that the earliest example that he could think of of a truly progressive group was that made up of the Gadarene swine.

Variant forms of the same word sometimes acquire different meanings and may then be regarded as different words. The unstressed form *to* has become a preposition while the stressed variant *too* has become an adverb. Similarly the adverb *off* is a stressed form of the preposition *of*, and *through* and *thorough* are both derived from OE *þurh*. The adjectival sense of *thorough* arose from the idea of going through something very efficiently, as when making a search. *Human* and *humane* have diverged, first in form and afterwards in meaning. From the eighteenth century *humane* began to be specialised to denote two of the most desirable attributes of human beings, the compassionate and the civilised; the latter sense is found in a phrase like 'humane studies'. Similarly *urban* and *urbane* both go back to Latin *urbanus*; *urban* is a colourless word meaning 'living in a town' while *urbane* is more specialised, denoting with approval the supposed qualities of those who live in towns. *Flour* and *flower* had the same meaning until *flour* was specialised to mean the finest part of the meal. *Courtesy* has kept the wide sense 'courteous behaviour' while its variant *curtsy* has been specialised to denote one of many acts by which courteous behaviour is exemplified. *Posy* is a variant of *poesy* and was applied to the motto engraved inside a ring; by metonymy it came to mean a small bunch of flowers. *Mettle* 'quality of temperament' is a variant of *metal* used metaphorically. The first element of *mantelpiece* is a specialised use of *mantle*; both words are from Latin *mantellum* 'cloak'. The earliest meaning of *travail* in English was 'pangs of childbirth'; already in Middle English its variant *travel* had come to mean 'to make a journey' because travelling is hard work. *Master* has the variant *Mr*, and *mistress* has given *Miss*, *Mrs* and, more recently, *Ms*. The last form is favoured by some because it does not reveal whether the person referred to is married; the pronunciation [miz] is arbitrary. *Born* and *borne* are variant forms of the past participle of *bear*, their meanings reflecting two meanings of the verb; *borne* means 'carried' while *born* means 'brought forth as offspring'. Other examples of divergence are *draught* and *draft*, *sergeant* and *serjeant*, *spirit* and *sprite*, and *gentle* and *genteel*.

Divergence can result from difference of stress, as in *dragon* and *dragoon*; the latter word is specialised from the use of *dragon* in French to denote a type of carbine so called because it breathed fire. Difference of stress is one of the causes of divergence between *saloon* and *salon*. Meaning can be changed by a change of suffix, as in *temporal* and *temporary*, which were at one time synonymous; today *temporal* is contrasted with *spiritual* while *temporary* means 'lasting for a limited time'.

CHAPTER SIX

Word Formation

Word formation is a branch of the study of language which might seem to have little to do with the affairs of everyday life, something that should be the concern of the grammarian but not of the man in the street, who hopes that if he leaves word formation alone it will leave him alone, but it is not a subject that we can afford to ignore. By paying attention to parts of words as well as complete words we can add to our vocabulary with little effort, because we can use and understand compound words and derivatives that we have never seen before, once we have understood the principles on which they are formed.

Words are convenient units in the division of a language into manageable parts, but in understanding a language we are concerned with sentences more than words and we use words chiefly to build up sentences. It is a natural development of this approach to language to remember that a word is not the smallest unit of meaning and that we can sometimes arrive at the meaning of a word by thinking about the meaning of its parts. G. W. Turner has considered the relative functions of the phrase, the word and the parts of a word:

> It is likely that many people think mainly in phrases, as we all do in all but strenuous conversations. 'Turned out nice again', 'We're none of us getting any younger', 'Well, I'll probably run into you again sometime soon', or 'Every teacher is a teacher of English' come ready made, and 'A chap at work was telling me the other day that fares are going up again', if not a single idiom, is pieced together out of two or three stereotyped parts. It is the educated writer who learns to think in words, weighing the contribution of each element in sequences which are

tailored to the occasion, enormously multiplying possible combinations of items by working with smaller parts. He depends on an educated reader able to think in the same way.

The scholar goes even further in becoming a skilled writer or reader by understanding the parts of words.[1]

COMPOUND WORDS

In compound words two words are linked to express a single idea without the loss of any part of either word. Such words are less common in the English of today than they were in Anglo-Saxon. They are common in German, but Latin and French have preferred to use phrases. It is often uncertain whether a pair of words should be regarded as one word or two. This uncertainty is reflected in writing by the three possibilities of joining up the two elements, writing them as two words and linking them with a hyphen. In speech the best indication that a pair of elements is regarded as a compound is that it receives a single main stress. *Blackberry* is pronounced with the stress on the first syllable but *black berry* is pronounced with level stress. The change to single stress often has an effect on the quality of the vowel in the lightly-stressed element, as in *cupboard*, and the same word illustrates the consonant-changes that are liable to take place when two elements are pronounced without a pause, the group [pb] being assimilated and simplified to [b]. The cause of the fusion of the two elements into a compound generally lies in the meaning: if the two elements denote a single object, they are likely to be regarded as a compound.

The most common type of compound is that in which the first element modifies the meaning of the second, as in *blackberry*, *bookcase* and *goldfish*. In such words the hyphen is most likely to be dropped. It remains in compounds, like *dug-out* and *lean-to*, where the second element does not bear the chief meaning of the word. Another fairly common type of compound is that where the first element is a verb and the second its object. Such words tend to be disparaging, like *scarecrow*, *killjoy*, *spitfire*, *pickpocket* and *makeshift*. One type of compound is the adjective made up of an adjective, a noun and the suffix *-ed*, as in *open-handed* and *foul-mouthed*. Some compounds are verbal jingles, like *helter-skelter*, *hurly-burly* or *topsy-turvy*. Others are formed from phrases, like *devil-may-care*, *happy-go-lucky*, *rough-and-ready*, *matter-of-fact*, *man-of-war* and *son-in-law*. Whether such groups are compounds or not is best decided by examining how we form the plural. If the first element is so independent as to take an inflexion of its own, as in *sons-in-law* beside *son-in-laws*, the group has less claim to be regarded as a compound word. Suffixes may be added to words formed from phrases, as in *lackadaisical*, a word coined by Laurence Sterne to denote a languishing person who is always saying 'Lackaday'.

Compound words undergo sound-changes, and their origin as compounds may be forgotten. *Fret* is from OE *fretan* 'to devour', from OE *etan* 'to eat' with an intensive prefix. *Lord* is from OE *hlāfweard* 'bread-keeper', while *lady* is from OE *hlǣfdige* 'bread-kneader'. *Barn* is from OE *bere-ærn* 'barley-house'. *Bonfire* is from *bone* and *fire*. *Gossip* is from *God* and *sibb* 'related'. *Gospel* is from OE *gōd* 'good' and *spel* 'news'. *Hussy* is from *house* and *wife*. *Sheriff* is from *shire* and *reeve*. *Daisy* is from *day's eye*. *Don* and *doff* are from *do on* and *do off*. Some compound words are from foreign phrases, like *alarm* (OFr *alarme*, from Italian *all'arme*), *carouse* (German *gar aus*) and *jeopardy* (OFr *jeu parti* 'even game'). Some otherwise obsolete words remain as parts of compound words. OE *gār* 'spear' survives in *garlic* (OE *gār-lēac* 'spear leek' from the shape of the leaves). *Stirrup* is from OE *stīg-rāp*, related to *stīgan* 'to climb'. It was the rope that you used when mounting a horse. *Handywork* is not derived from *handy*; the *y* is from OE *ge-*, a collective prefix in the second element *geweorc*. *Handicraft* owes its *i* to the influence of *handywork*.

Many words in various languages incorporate a preceding article, and some of them have been borrowed into English. *Alligator* is from Spanish *el lagarto* 'the lizard' and *lariat* from *la reata* 'the rope'. *Lacrosse* is from French *(le jeu de) la crosse* '(the game of) the hooked stick', where *la* is the French definite article. *Daffodil* is from Dutch *de affodil*, with the noun borrowed through French from Latin *asphodelus*. The Arabic *al* is found in a large number of words, such as *alchemy*, *alcohol*, *alcove*, *algebra*, *alkali* and *almanac*, and in disguised forms in *apricot* (Fr *abricot*, from Portuguese *albricoque*) and *elixir*, borrowed through Medieval Latin from Arabic *al iksir* 'the medicinal powder'.

It is usually left to the hearer to work out the exact relation between the two elements of a compound, and sometimes the answer is uncertain. *Anglo-Indian* is sometimes used to denote an Englishman living and working in India, but it sometimes means the offspring of a mixed marriage. An illustration of the changes which the lapse of time can produce in the use of words was provided by a well-informed student who said that English rule in India had come to an end so long before she was born that she did not remember hearing the word in any sense.

There are varying degrees of closeness in the two elements. In *daisy* junction is complete. In *blackbird* it is fairly close, as is shown by the accent. In *matter-of-fact* it is loose, as is shown by the hyphens. In most compounds the normal grammatical function of one of the elements is changed.

English has a large number of verbal phrases, which are written as two words though they have much in common with compound words. Common verbs like *give*, *let* and *set* combine with adverbs to form verbal phrases like *give in*, *let down* and *set aside*. As in compounds, the relation between the verb and the adverb can vary considerably. These verbal phrases have sometimes coalesced to form compounds like *undergo* and *withstand*.

PREFIXES AND SUFFIXES

Prefixes and suffixes can have a life of their own, as when we speak of 'fascism, racism or any other -isms', but many of them have come to be regarded as inseparable from the rest of the word of which they form a part. For example, *dis-* is a common prefix, but it is only as a joke that anyone would say 'He may not have been disgruntled but he was far from gruntled'. There are, however, several prefixes and suffixes which can be used at will to form new words whose meaning will be clear even to those who have never heard them before. These affixes are said to be living. Examples are the prefixes *re-*, *un-* and *non-* and the suffixes *-ness*, *-ise*, *-ist*, *-ish* and *-able*, found in such words as *rethink*, *undeniable*, *non-existent*, *darkness*, *macadamise*, *racist*, *childish* and *bearable*, whereas the suffix *-th*, as in *length*, is no longer living. The addition of a suffix often makes a word pejorative. *Sentimentality* is less attractive than *sentiment*, and a reader of Jane Austen knows that *sense* is better than *sensibility*. If a word acquires too many affixes, people are liable to complain of its length, as A. P. Herbert did of such words as *decontaminate*, much used during the Second World War. There have at various times been attempts to discover the longest word in the English language. Before the discovery of organic compounds with immensely long names, the favourite candidate was *antidisestablishmentarianism*, a word for which there is little need, consisting almost wholly of prefixes and suffixes.

Just as no two words are exact synonyms, no two prefixes are exactly alike in sense. Even if they begin with the same meaning, they undergo divergent development in different words to establish a distinction which speakers find useful and which hearers may or may not understand or accept, as in *uninterested* 'not interested' compared with *disinterested* 'impartial'. Similarly suffixes can develop in different ways: *womanish* is pejorative but *womanly* is not. Some suffixes of foreign origin are especially common in scientific terms, and the existence of two different suffixes may be useful. For example, *ferrous* means 'containing iron in divalent form' but *ferric* means 'containing iron in trivalent form'. There are many such pairs in non-scientific use which serve as traps for the unwary. *Dialectal* means 'connected with dialect' but *dialectical* means 'connected with logical disputation'; *geography* and *geology* are concerned with different aspects of the earth, and *biology* and *biography* with life in two of its senses.

Prefixes different in origin and meaning have fallen together. The prefix *in-* indicates movement towards in such words as *influx*, *ingredient*, *insight* and *intrude*, but there is also a negative prefix *in-*, found in *inedible*, *insane*, *insoluble* and *invisible*. Two other prefixes that are sometimes confused are *for-*, indicating prohibition or abstention, as in *forbear*, *forget* and *forgive*, and *fore-* meaning 'before', as in *foresee* and *forehead*.

In Old English the prefixes *for-*, *with-* and *un-* were particularly productive, but they have sometimes been replaced by prefixes of foreign origin. For example, *withspeak* has been replaced by *contradict*. Another prefix that used to be more common than it is today is *be-*, used to make intransitive verbs transitive, as in *behowl* and *bespeak*, and *mid-* 'with', which survives in *midwife*.

The addition of a prefix may preserve an older meaning of the word to which it is prefixed. King Ethelred II is traditionally known as Ethelred the Unready, not because he was always late for his appointments but because he was ill-advised. In Old English *rǣd* meant 'wisdom' or 'counsel' and the nickname *Unred* provided a jingle with the king's name: Ethelred literally means 'noble counsel' while *Unred* means 'evil counsel'.

When the function of a prefix is forgotten, the prefix is sometimes re-introduced in an emphatic form and this may lead to a difference of meaning, as in *resign* and *re-sign*, *recover* and *re-cover*. The hyphen is the convention of the written language which reflects the extra stress given to the prefix in the spoken language.

Some suffixes can be either active or passive. *Gaol* and *prison* are near-synonyms, but the addition of the suffix *-er* produces two words of contrasted meaning: a *gaoler* looks after a prison but a *prisoner* is looked after. Similarly *laborious* is applied to the work but *industrious* to the worker. In course of time suffixes may pass from an active to a passive meaning or vice versa. In Shakespeare *fearful* meant 'inspiring fear' but today it means 'feeling fear'. The Thane of Cawdor gave up his life 'as 'twere a careless trifle' (*Macbeth*, I.4.11), that is, as if it were something not worth caring about. *Tuneable* in Shakespeare meant 'tuneful' (*A Midsummer Night's Dream*, I.1.184) and Orlando described Rosalind as 'The fair, the chaste, and unexpressive she' (*As You Like It*, III.2.10), meaning that she was inexpressibly beautiful.

The meanings of suffixes can change with time and circumstance, such as colloquial use. The suffix *-ish* is commonly used in standard English to form adjectives from nouns, as in *boyish*. When added to other parts of speech it creates words that are colloquial or slang, such as *stand-offish*, *uppish* and *sixish*. As an indicator of approximation it has been used on a clock-face without a minute-hand and with the numerals replaced by *oneish, twoish* and so on. This is surely carrying diffidence too far.

During the last two centuries there has been much discussion of abstract political theories, which has led to the creation of a large number of abstract nouns formed from nouns or adjectives by the addition of the suffix *-ism*: *despotism, terrorism, socialism, communism, collectivism, militarism, pacifism, opportunism*. These abstract nouns all have corresponding nouns in *-ist* to denote anyone who adopts those doctrines. Impatience with theorising has caused these words to be chiefly pejorative.

Sometimes prefixes and suffixes have been fused so completely with the rest of the word that they are hard to recognise. The initial *s-* of *sport* is all that is left of the prefix found in OFr *desporter* literally 'to carry away'; *sport* is an aphetic form of *disport*, which means something that carries you out of yourself. Suffixes are even more liable to be absorbed into a word, with the result that their origin is forgotten. The *th* in *warmth* is the descendant of a once-common suffix used to form abstract nouns from adjectives. It originally had an *i* before the *th* which often changed the stem-vowel, thus further disguising the connexion between the adjective and the noun in such pairs as *long* and *length*, *strong* and *strength*, *broad* and *breadth*. Other common suffixes can still be used to form new words. Abstract nouns can be formed from verbs and adjectives by the addition of *-ment*, as in *judgement*, *acknowledgement*, and *merriment*. The suffixes *-able* and *-ible* are used to form adjectives from verbs; such adjectives are usually passive, like *breakable* and *legible*, but occasionally active, like *sensible*. *Laughable* and *reliable* have been condemned because they are formed from verbs which are used with a preposition. The French suffix *-ée* was originally the ending of a past participle with passive force and is so used in such words as *employee* and *nominee*, but it is also used more widely, as in *absentee* and *refugee*. The native suffix *-lāc*, common in Old English but rare today, survives in *wedlock*; *-ness*, *-dom* and *-hood* occur in words that are still widely used, and a new formation like *stardom* causes no surprise. The French suffix *-ous* is used to form adjectives from nouns, as in *capricious* and *murderous*. The suffixes *-al* and *-age* are used to form nouns from verbs, as in *betrothal* and *marriage*. Latin verbs are normally borrowed from the present stem, but a number have been borrowed from the past participle and so end in *-ate*, as in *discriminate* and *accumulate*. The suffix *-y* to form adjectives from nouns has not been completely accepted, and *wealthy* is regarded by some as substandard; *pricey* is a slang euphemism for 'expensive' and *wordy* is pejorative. The suffix *-ado* sounds Spanish but in most of the words in which it occurs it is probably a sonorous refashioning of some other suffix; it is found in such words as *desperado*, *bravado*, *bastinado* and *strappado*.[2]

Because of functional shift there is less use of suffixes in English today than in the past; instead of using a suffix to form one part of speech from another, we generally prefer to use the original form unchanged.

POPULAR ETYMOLOGY

Popular etymology, sometimes called folk etymology, is the modification of the form of a word to make it seem to be derived from a word with more familiar components than those occurring in the word from which it was in fact derived. It results from confusion between components which resemble each other in sound but which are not related etymologically. Such mistaken associations are probably very common but as a rule they remain undetected; it is only when the mistake is reflected in spelling or pronunciation that popular etymology becomes recognisable. Many people think that *reindeer* has some connexion with *rein* and they often have a picture in their minds of Santa Claus being drawn by deer controlled by reins, but the resemblance between the two words is accidental. The rein of a horse is from OFr *reigne*, while the first element of *reindeer* is from ON *hreinn* 'reindeer'; the second element is from OE *dēor* 'animal', and the development to 'deer' is a well-known example of restriction of meaning. Before the restriction was completely established, compounding with *rein* was a useful way of indicating which restriction was intended.

Popular etymology is not always the work of uneducated speakers. It was the learned who changed the spelling of *rime* (OE *rīm*) to *rhyme* because they associated the word with *rhythm* and of *sisoures* (OFr *cisoires*) to *scissors* by association with Latin *scindere*.

Popular etymology is often applied to loan-words to make them resemble familiar native words, as in the substandard *sparrow grass* for *asparagus*, borrowed from Latin. Problems arise when words borrowed from a foreign language contain sounds which do not occur in the language into which the word is borrowed. Speakers with a knowledge of the language from which the word comes will at first keep the foreign pronunciation, but most speakers will resort to sound-substitution, the replacement of the foreign sound by its nearest native equivalent, with the result that *fête* is pronounced like *fate* and the first syllable of *envelope* is pronounced like *on*. A later stage is to ignore the original pronunciation altogether and to give the word a spelling pronunciation. The imitation of a foreign pronunciation may produce a sound which is difficult to understand or remember and there is always a temptation to modify the pronunciation to make it resemble that of an English word, even if there is no similarity in meaning. These are the conditions in which folk etymology flourishes. British soldiers on the Continent in two world wars produced their own versions of everyday French words and phrases. *Vin blanc* became *plonk*, *tout de suite* became *toot sweet* and *camouflage* became *camel flags*.

There is often little connexion in meaning between the two words that are linked by popular etymology. Logan Pearsall Smith makes this point:

> This method of punning or popular etymology often leads to somewhat absurd results, for any kind of meaning, however inappropriate, will do, so long as there is a similarity of sound. The word, it is felt, must mean something, even if the meaning have no connection with the object or process which it describes.[3]

'Popular etymology' is not an altogether happy term to denote what takes place, because it suggests that the speaker has assumed that the malformation that he adopts is an etymology. In fact most of those who introduce such malformations are not really interested in etymology at all, as may be seen by the frequent incongruity in meaning of the whole word with the newly-created element.

Sometimes an etymology is provided for one syllable while the rest of the word is left to take care of itself. Association with other words can bring about a slight change in the form or spelling of a word. *Debt* (OFr *dette*), *doubt* (OFr doute) and *subtle* (OFr *sotil*) owe their *b* to the reconstruction of their ultimate Latin etymons *debitum*, *dubito* and *subtilis*, but the *b* has not crept into the pronunciation. In *perfect* (OFr *perfet*), *verdict* (AN *verdit*) and *subject* (OFr *suget*) a *c* has been introduced by Latin influence into both spelling and pronunciation, and for a similar reason *l* has re-appeared in *fault*, *assault* and *cauldron*. These re-introductions do not result from any misconception about the origin of the words in which they occur; they merely show a preference for the ultimate to the immediate etymology. There have, however, been some modifications of spelling resulting from mistakes, such as the common early English spelling *abhominable*, which arose from the mistaken idea that the word came from the Latin *ab homine*, and the introduction of *l* into *could* by the influence of *should* and *would*. *Island* (OE *īgland*) gained its *s* by the influence of OFr *isle* from Latin *insula*.

When characters in novels and plays indulge in popular etymology they produce malapropisms, the conversions of unfamiliar words into others more familiar. Mrs Quickly converts *homicidal* into *honeysuckle* and *homicide* into *honeyseed* (*2 Henry IV*, II.1. 48, 50).

Sound-changes can conceal the real etymology of a word and give a false impression without any misunderstanding on the part of the speaker. *Pantry* has nothing to do with pans but much to do with bread (OFr *paneterie*, cf. Latin *panis*), and *buttery* is connected with *butt* 'cask' rather than with butter.

Blend or portmanteau words are formed by combining some of the sounds from two different words, each word contributing something to both sound and meaning of the new word. Many words which cautious lexicographers describe as being of obscure etymology may have arisen in this way, but there is room for conjecture about the exact words which form the basis of such coinages. Lewis Carroll coined a number of blend words in his poem *Jabberwocky*, and in the Preface to *The Hunting of the Snark* he explained what words he had blended: *slithy* came from *lithe* and *slimy*, *mimsy* from *flimsy* and *miserable*. More recent blends are *brunch* from *breakfast* and *lunch*, *motel* from *motor* and *hotel* and *smog* from *smoke* and *fog*.

Some examples may be given of the operation of popular etymology in English words:

admiral is from OFr *amiral* and ultimately from Arabic *amir* 'commander'. The *d* is due to confusion, found already in Old French, with the Latin adjective *admirabilis*.

belfry is from OFr *berfrei*, a word of Germanic origin meaning 'place of safety'. The bells came later.

by-law is a regulation made by a local authority, and the first element, of Scandinavian origin, is a common element in place-names, such as *Whitby*. Popular etymology has not affected the form of the word, but many people think that the first element is the preposition *by*.

catsup has nothing to do with cats. It is a variant of *ketchup* and is from a Chinese word, used in Malaya, meaning 'the brine of pickled fish'.

causeway. The first element is from Old North French *cauciee*, cognate with Modern French *chaussée*. The form *causey* is still common in Modern English dialects and in standard English has been blended with *way*.

cockroach is from Spanish *cucaracha*, modified in form to make it resemble the English words *cock* and *roach*.

crayfish is from OFr *crevis*, blended with English *fish*.

cutlet is from OFr *costelette*, a diminutive of *coste* 'rib' but it has been assimilated to the verb *cut*.

gillyflower is from OFr *girofle* blended with *flower*.

helpmate was probably an attempt to make sense of *helpmeet*, which arose from a misunderstanding of 'I will make him an help meet for him' (that is, 'suitable for him') in Genesis 2.18.

hiccough shows the influence of the spelling of *cough* on the echoic word *hiccup*, but the pronunciation has not been affected.

isinglass is from Dutch *huysenblas* 'sturgeon's bladder' assimilated to English *glass*.

Jerusalem artichoke is from Italian *girasole* 'turning with the sun' and Italian *articiocco*. Both words have been modified; the first has been replaced by a place-name and the second has been influenced by *choke*.

lanyard is a blend of OFr *laniere* and English *yard*.

mandrake is from OFr *mandragore*, influenced by the obsolete English *drake* 'dragon'.

mongoose is from Marathi *mangus*. Its assimilation to *goose* has occasionally caused it to be given an erroneous plural.

parsnip is a blend of OFr *pasnaie* and OE *nǣp* 'turnip', which survives in the second syllable of *turnip*.

pennyroyal is from AN *puliol real*, with translation of the second word and rather drastic assimilation of the first word to *penny*.

penthouse is from OFr *apentis*, from Latin *appendicium* 'appendage'. The final syllable has been assimilated to *house*.

rosemary is from Latin *ros marinus* 'sea-dew', slightly modified by *rose* and *Mary*.

salt-cellar. The second element has no connexion with the underground room which we call a cellar. It is from OFr *saliere*, a derivative of Latin *sal* 'salt'. When the origin of the word was forgotten, *salt* was added redundantly to make the meaning clear.

shamefaced is from OE *sceamfæst*. The second element meant 'firmly fixed', as when we speak of fast colours, and the whole word was a term of praise meaning 'modest'. Association with *face* changed the meaning of the word for the worse to 'showing shame on one's face'.

sovereign is from OFr *souverain*, but it acquired a *g* by association with *reign* and *foreign*.

standard is from OFr *estendart* and is related to *extend*. Association with *stand* has affected both spelling and meaning, since we think of a standard as something fixed, with which variables can be compared.

surround is from AN *sur(o)under* and is a derivative of Latin *unda* 'wave'. It has been influenced in meaning by association with *round*.

syllable is from AN *sillable*, altered from OFr *sillabe* by association with the large number of words ending in *-able*.

tongue is from OE *tunge* and it acquired its *u* by the influence of words of French origin like *vague* and *catalogue*.

touchy is probably derived from *tetchy* 'easily irritated', from OFr *tecche* 'spot, blemish', influenced by *touch*.

The second element of *turtledove* is redundant, since *turtle* is from Latin *turtur* 'dove'. The element *dove* was added to distinguish the word from the name of the marine tortoise.

walnut originally had no connexion with *wall*. It is from OE *wealh* 'foreign' and is related to *Welsh*.

wiseacre, from Middle Dutch *wijsseggher*, has been influenced by *acre* in spite of the difference of meaning.

wormwood had originally no connexion with either *worm* or *wood*. It is from OE *wērmōd*, cognate with MnE *vermouth*, and the two syllables have been assimilated to *worm* and *wood*.

VARIOUS TYPES OF WORD FORMATION

Back-formation is the creation of a new base-form from a longer word which has the appearance of being derived from the new base-form. For example, *sidelong* is an adverb in which the suffix *-long* has replaced earlier *-ling* Back-formation took place when it was assumed that the suffix in *sideling* was the much more common *-ing* and that *sideling* was the present participate of a verb *to sidle*. Similarly, in the sixteenth century *grovelling* was an adverb meaning 'on the ground', hence 'abjectly'. In this word too *-ling* was confused with *-ing*, and so a new verb *to grovel* was formed. Both of these verbs have become accepted in standard English, but sometimes a feeling persists that the formation is not quite regular and the new word is regarded as slang. This has happened with the verb *to mizzle*, which had its origin in a misunderstanding of *misled*, the past participle of *mislead*. Some back-formations originate as deliberate jokes and never become anything else, like the verb *to frivol* 'to behave frivolously'.

The ending *-s* has given rise to a number of back-formations resulting from uncertainty whether it was or was not a plural ending. *Pea* and *cherry* have lost an *s* as a result of this confusion. *Pea* is from OE *pise* and the *s* is preserved in *peasecod* and *pease-pudding*, and *cherry* is from ONFr *cherise* (cf. Fr cerise). Similarly *burial* is from OE *byrgels*, *sherry* is from earlier *sherris*, from Spanish *(vino de) Xeres*, now Jerez, and *asset* is from OFr *asez* 'enough'. The reverse process is seen in *bodice*, from the plural of *body*, and *quince*, from the plural of an obsolete *quoyn*, ultimately from the place-name Cydonia in Crete. The back-formation *corp*, from *corpse*, has not passed beyond the realms of slang, and even there it is generally used facetiously.

Compound words can give rise to back-formations as a result of a misconception about the relation between the two elements. *Swash* is an echoic verb meaning 'to clash', a *buckler* is a small round shield and a *swashbuckler* is someone who makes a blustering noise by striking a shield with his sword. It was misunderstood as an agent noun and produced the verb *to swashbuckle*. *Henpecked* 'under the domination of one's wife' has given the verb *to henpeck*.

Curtailment has produced many back-formations, not all of which have passed into standard English. *Opine* is an affected verb which could be derived from Latin *opinari*, but it is probably to be regarded as a back-formation from *opinion*. Other verbs resulting from curtailment are *enthuse* (from *enthusiasm*), *orate* (from *orator*), *maffick* (from the place-name Mafeking), *edit* (from *editor*), *donate* (from *donation*), *televise* (from *television*) and *resurrect* (from *resurrection*). Some back-formations remain as slang without passing into standard English; they are used as mild jokes. Examples are *peeve* (from *peevish*), *to jell* (from *jelly*), *to buttle* (from *butler*) and *to diddle* (from Jeremy Diddler in James Kenney's *Raising the Wind*, 1803).

A process that has something in common with back-formation is the creation of new words by the misdivision of words, sometimes accompanied by the reduction of the misdivided word as a result of lack of stress. In *tawdry*, *saint* has been reduced to its final consonant which has been joined to the following word. St Audrey, or Etheldrida, was the patron saint of Ely, and at the fair held in remembrance of her St Audrey's lace was sold. Those who disapproved of this lace then used *tawdry* to describe cheap or tasteless finery.

The most common kind of misdivision is that in which the consonant *n* plays a part, and it results from the existence of two forms of the indefinite article, *a* before a consonant and *an* before a vowel. We find two groups of words, one consisting of words beginning with *n* which they have acquired from a preceding *an* and the other consisting of words which once began with *n* but which now begin with a vowel. To the first group belong *newt* (OE *efeta*) and

nickname (from ME ***eke-name***, cf. OE ***ēac*** 'also'); to the second group belong ***umpire*** (ME ***noumpere***, from OFr ***nonper*** 'not equal'), ***adder*** (OE ***nǣdre***), ***apron*** (ME ***naperon***, from a diminutive of OFr ***nape*** 'tablecloth') and ***orange*** (OFr ***orenge*** ultimately from Arabic ***naranj***). In one word the initial ***n***- comes from an inflected form of a preceding definite article, which is no longer inflected: ***nonce*** in the phrase 'for the nonce' and in the compound ***nonce-word*** 'a word that occurs only once' is from ME ***for then anes*** 'for the time being'. *Ninny* 'simpleton' may be by misdivision from ***an innocent***. Misdivision has given us a place-name in *Riding*, one of the three regions into which Yorkshire was historically divided; it is from ON ***þriðjungr*** 'third part'.

Curtailment has played a significant part in the development of English words. *Gent*, from ***gentleman***, and ***quack***, from ***quacksalver***, occur before the seventeenth century. Curtailment was common as a fashionable affectation at the time of Queen Anne, giving such words as ***hipped*** 'depressed' from ***hypochondria***, ***incog*** for ***incognito***, ***plenipo*** for ***plenipotentiary*** and *cit* for ***citizen***. There have been many later examples, such as *curio(sity)*, ***piano(forte)***, ***miss*** for ***mistress*** and ***gin*** from Dutch ***genever***. Sheard points out[4] that names of drinks are particularly liable to be shortened: ***brandy*** for ***brandy wine***, ***whisky*** for ***usquebaugh***, ***grog*** for ***grogram***, ***hock*** for ***Hochheimer***, ***port*** for ***Oporto*** and ***rum*** for ***rumbullion***. Other shortenings are ***zoo***, ***pram*** and ***bus***. Some are not generally recognised as shortenings; examples are ***sport*** for ***disport***, ***cab*** for ***cabriolet***, ***chap*** for ***chapman***, ***wig*** for ***periwig*** and ***fan*** for ***fanatic***.

Latin phrases are sometimes shortened. The most familiar example is ***mob*** for ***mobile vulgus*** but there are several examples of the reduction of phrases to single words, as in ***quorum***, originally the first word of the instructions to JPs specifying the minimum number required for proceedings to be valid. *Affidavit* 'he has stated on oath' is the first word of a sworn statement. ***Subpoena*** 'under penalty' is the first word of a charge to a witness to attend under penalty for failure. *Veto* 'I forbid' is the first word of the Latin formula by which a sovereign withholds his consent to the act of a minister. Some words are curtailed in the colloquial language of particular groups, like the schoolboy's *prep*, *exam*, *maths* and *trig*, the university student's *vac* and the sportsman's *soccer*. The curtailment may be better known than its original. Many of those who speak of a *navvy* do not realise that the word is a shortened form of a *navigator*, who dug canals. When both the original and the curtailed form continue to exist, there is usually a divergence of meaning, as in *(a)cute*, *(a)mend* and *(de)fence*.

Curtailment is common in regional dialects, as in *liver* for *deliver* and *divvy* for *dividend*. A vicar's servant said that he worked too hard, 'but his desk 'tices him'. During the Second World War an evacuee expressed his alarm at the reluctance of households to accept his friends: 'We've nobbut 'livered three this morning'.

When polysyllabic words are shortened, it is natural that the accented syllables should have the best chance of survival, and in English these are likely to be the first. Thus *submarine* becomes *sub* and *public house* becomes *pub*, but when the first syllable is unstressed it is usually lost, as in *(es)cheat*, *(with)drawing-room*, *(di)sport* and *sample* from *example*. *Bus*, from *omnibus*, is exceptional in several ways. Not only is it an unaccented syllable which has survived but the surviving syllable, which is part of an inflexional ending, gives no indication of the meaning of the word, which has been remarkably tenacious of life, occurring in many European languages. In general the curtailments that have survived best are those dealing with everyday life, such as *pub*, *phone* and *taxi*.

One of the most common kinds of curtailment is aphesis, the loss of a short unaccented vowel at the beginning of a word. It has been taking place from time to time ever since the early Middle English period. *Spice*, from OFr *espice*, is recorded from the thirteenth century. *Cute*, from *acute*, is much later, being used in England in the sense 'clever' from the eighteenth century and in America in the sense 'attractive' from the nineteenth. The origin of the musical term *chord*, an aphetic form of *accord*, is disguised by the spelling with an intrusive *h*. As usual when new words arise from a sound-change, doublets develop, with divergence of meaning as well as spelling between the old form and the new. *Size*, from *assize*, originally meant 'ordinance' but it came to mean 'fixed standard' and then 'magnitude'. *Ticket* is from *etiquette* and the original meaning is preserved in the colloquial 'That's the ticket'. *Venture* is from *adventure* and probably arose from confusion between the prefix *a-* and the indefinite article, especially in the phrase *at adventure*. *Vie* is from OFr *envier* 'to outbid' and is therefore related to *envy*.

One source of new words that has been very productive in recent years is the use of acronyms, words formed from the initial letters of other words. If the initials form a pronounceable word, it replaces the initials, as in *Wren* for Women's Royal Naval Service and *Naafi* for Navy, Army and Air Force Institutes. Our willingness to accept the initials as a word depends not only on ease of pronunciation but also on frequency of use. We have heard so much of NATO (North Atlantic Treaty Organisation) that we accept *Nato* as a new word, but we have not shown a similar readiness to accept *Seato* (South-East Asia Treaty Organisation). We have accepted *Unesco* (United Nations Educational, Scientific and Cultural Organisation), whose activities are nearer home. Phrases so long that they would have no chance of acceptance in their unabbreviated form sometimes seem to be coined to produce acronyms. We should probably have heard less of quasi-autonomous, non-governmental organisations if the term had not been abbreviated to *quangos*. Debate in Parliament has revealed that there were at one time nine hundred national or regional quangos in the United Kingdom, and many people believe that their number 'has increased, is increasing and ought to be diminished'. There is some uncertainty about the meaning of the word, some people taking the *ng* to stand for 'non-governmental' while others take it to mean 'national governmental'. Between the two *quango* could be held to cover most forms of human activity, and uncertainty about the meaning may lead to the early death of the word, in spite of its attractive sound.

CHAPTER SEVEN

Language and Literature

For reasons that seemed to me adequate at the time, I once tried to translate into Anglo-Saxon the regulations of a university department of English. I then made the salutary discovery that it was difficult to find an Anglo-Saxon word for 'literature' that did not also mean 'language'. The supposed rift between language and literature is one about which much has been heard in universities during the last century, but today there are welcome signs that we are returning to a conception of literature in which language plays an important part. Language is used for a number of purposes, such as conversation, buying a bus ticket or making a will, that have nothing to do with literature, but literature without language is inconceivable. Such a view does not exalt the importance of language at the expense of literature. Painting without pigments is inconceivable, but we are in no doubt about the relative importance of painting and pigments; so far as the register of literature is concerned, language is the material of which literature is made. To the man in the street the picture is different. For him language is primarily a speaking activity to be supplemented by writing to an extent which varies with his job. Literature is one of the many activities for which he uses language, and it may occupy an important place in his life or no place at all.

It is easy to think of ways in which a knowledge of language and its history can enhance the appreciation of literature. If the characters in a novel 'talk like a book', it is likely that they are using the wrong register, and a novelist or a dramatist needs to be conscious of the difference between spoken and written language. To appreciate the use of archaisms in poetry it is necessary to know whether apparent archaisms are the result of linguistic changes that have taken place since the poem was written or whether they were already archaic when the poet wrote. In a single scene of a Shakespearean play characters will vary between the use of *thou* and *you* in an apparently aimless way, but the linguist can see that the variation is not aimless; it provides information about the fluctuating relationships between the two characters who are taking part in the exchanges. But apart from these matters of detail, the whole question of the use of figurative language, which underlies virtually every word in a work of literature, can be regarded as both a linguistic and a literary problem. The figurative language used by a poet is simply a heightened form of that used in everyday life by a man unconscious that he is using any such language. It is possible to study subjects such as metre or figures of speech from either a literary or a linguistic point of view, and the most profitable study is one which combines both approaches.

It is often said that a poem or a good piece of prose cannot be paraphrased effectively, because the paraphrase is usually inferior to the original, but the practice can be defended because the literal meaning of the words used is one element that the reader should be expected to recognise before he turns his attention to the poetic devices. Paraphrase serves a useful purpose in showing how small a part a literal statement contributes to the effect of a poem. Paraphrase can show the value of what cannot be paraphrased. Robert Graves and Alan Hodge, in *The Reader over your Shoulder*, call attention to the shortcomings of a number of prose passages by well-known authors and then rewrite them in what they believe to be correct English. After reading these paraphrases, a reader is conscious of a feeling of flatness and he turns back with relief to the supposedly faulty originals. Helen Waddell, one of the authors whose work is discussed, felt more strongly. The authors report:

> We are sorry to say that she disagrees strongly with our comments, rejects the fair copy as 'singularly inaccurate, verbose and silly', and maintains that the original context makes the meaning of the passage perfectly clear.[1]

Some critics resort to *explication de texte*, which involves a close examination and analysis of vocabulary and syntax, including the figures of speech and the rhythm, of a passage of adequate length. Critics of this school try to transpose the artistic activity of the writer, which is individual and personal, into a language that can be studied objectively. In doing so they are in danger of missing what gives the original text its value.

Much of the material printed in books and newspapers has been written hurriedly for readers who will skim over it hurriedly. To subject such material to careful analysis is breaking a butterfly on a wheel. Unfortunately the habit of hasty reading is not easily broken, and when we turn to works of literary value we tend to read them too quickly. The careful reading advocated by the devotee of *explication de texte* is a useful beginning, but it leaves untouched a number of things that do not lend themselves to objective analysis. Analysis does not show how the various elements of literary language interpenetrate one another, with the result that a literary work is more than the sum of its parts. Chief of the elements of a literary work that react on one another are sound and sense.

There is no essential difference between the language of poetry and that of everyday life. Both the poet and the man in the street use imagery, but the poet is more free to experiment in the use of language without being accused of extravagance. On the other hand, the poet conforms to certain self-imposed limitations, such as rhyme and metre. The reader sometimes has a sense of frustration when he feels that a writer is using the wrong medium, as when he finds that large parts of the prose in Sheridan's *Pizarro* can be scanned as blank verse or when, in reading Browning, he is reminded of Oscar Wilde's gibe 'Meredith is a prose Browning, and so is Browning.'

In writings that make no claim to be considered as works of literature devices that are generally thought of as literary are used in order to add point to a criticism or to introduce an element of surprise by making a statement whose significance becomes clear only after a few moments' thought. I think that it was a physicist who said that the sciences fall into two broad divisions, physics and stamp-collecting. He might have made the point more soberly by saying that many scientists are unduly preoccupied with the acquisition and classification of specimens, but the apparently irrelevant mention of stamp-collecting startles the reader and revives his flagging attention by the use of metaphor.

Classification of the various figures of speech has a long history and it has produced a large number of technical terms whose use is liable to cause resentment today. The most legitimate objection to their use is that it is too easy to give an impression of learning by producing a large number of technical terms to denote figures that are in fact quite simple. Molière's M Jourdain had been using prose all his life without realising it, and he would have been even more gratified to be assured that he had also been using metonymy, synecdoche and hysteron proteron. There is no need to use a technical term for a figure of speech unless it occurs fairly often. If it does, the technical term is a useful piece of shorthand in spite of its exotic appearance, but there is good sense in Geoffrey Leech's reminder that 'knowing the actual names is of minimal importance compared with understanding the realities they denote'.[2]

Both poets and prose-writers sometimes give way to the temptation to play tricks with language by the excessive use of figures of speech. In doing so they may be indulging in parody of a current fashion or simply giving way to a whim. There are examples of excessive alliteration in Shakespeare, such as 'The preyful princess pierc'd and prick'd a pretty pleasing pricket' (*Love's Labour's Lost*, IV.2.52) or 'Whereat with blade, with bloody blameful blade, He bravely broach'd his boiling bloody breast' (*A Midsummer Night's Dream*, V.1.146). There are unexpected rhymes, such as *fabric*: *dab brick* in Browning's *Grammarian's Funeral* and *philosopher*: *gloss over* in *Hudibras*. Such excesses tend to be the stylistic tricks of particular authors and sometimes seem to be examples of self-parody.

By far the most important figure of speech, in both literature and everyday life, is metaphor, a name-transfer based on resemblance, which involves speaking of an object in terms of something else. Metaphors are most effective when the two things compared are in some ways strikingly different as well as having enough points of resemblance to make the metaphor possible. The statement that a rose looks like another flower may be true but it is not interesting; it does not give the satisfaction of surprise that we feel when a ballet dancer says that his job is that of a fork-lift truck. We feel the same sort of satisfaction when a simile takes two things which seem to have nothing in common and then goes on to show that the comparison is quite reasonable. Some authors have a special fondness for these seemingly fanciful comparisons, like this example from a modern novel:

> The motions of collation recall those of watching fast tennis. Since two columns of print are to be compared with each other not merely word by word but letter by letter, the eyes (and also, perceptibly, the head) must be flicked from side to side with metronomic regularity.[3]

The comparison is developed with perhaps unnecessary detail, but another comparison is introduced more concisely by the single word 'metronomic' in the last line.

The use of metaphor in poetry is an extension of its use in everyday life. The metaphors that we use in ordinary conversation tend to be dead or dying; the poet can show greater originality in his use of metaphor and so extend the language at his disposal. The point has been made by Winifred Nowottny:

> To look at metaphor as a linguistic phenomenon is to begin to suspect that the basic explanation of the prevalence of metaphor in poetry lies in the fact that metaphor, by extending the range of terminology at the poet's disposal, offers him a magnificent array of solutions to major problems of diction.[4]

Metaphors enable a poet to appeal to readers who are insensitive to one kind of sensory perception by substituting another kind. Thus we get synaesthetic imagery. A man who is more sensitive to variations of heat or cold than to those of colour will appreciate the metaphor 'a warm colour' and one whose ear is more sensitive than his eye will understand the meaning of 'a loud suit'. Another kind of metaphor is that based on what has been called the pathetic fallacy. Metaphors of this kind attribute human emotions to inanimate objects and cause us to speak of 'the friendly sunshine' or 'an angry sky'. To give liveliness, verbs of physical action are used to denote activities that are not physical. We run into debt, fall in love and fly into a passion. When the reluctance of readers to buy books in paper covers is at last overcome, lovers of excitable language are liable to describe the change in taste as the paperback revolution.

There is often humorous intent in the use of a metaphor, as when a man who moves stealthily is called a *pussyfoot* or when an artist's *easel* is so called because, like a donkey, it bears a burden. A *tandem* is a pair of horses one in front of the other and later a bicycle made for two. To *patter* is to repeat the paternoster or other prayers rapidly or glibly, and *patter* is then used as a noun to denote the talk of a cheap-jack. A *pot-boiler* is a book written to provide its author with the necessaries of life.

We become conscious of mixed metaphors when writer and reader are not equally conscious of the extent to which a metaphor is still alive. When Lady Macbeth asks 'Was the hope drunk, Wherein you dress'd yourself? hath it slept since, And wakes it now, to look so green and pale At what it did so freely?' (*Macbeth*, I.7.35), her mind passes so quickly from one image to the next that she is unconscious of the incongruity that her words may present to a hearer who remains conscious of the literal, as well as the metaphorical, meaning of the words she uses.

Most figures of speech are based on resemblance, but there are some figures that are based not on similarity but on contiguity, either physical or mental. In synecdoche the name of the part is applied to the whole or that of the whole to the part, as when we speak of employees as *hands* or of a motor-car as a *motor*. Another figure based on contiguity is metonymy, where the name of an object is used to denote anything that has some connexion with it. It may be the material of which the object is made, as when we use *glass* to mean 'drinking-glass' or *glasses* to mean 'spectacles', or it may be an attribute used to denote the people who possess it, as when we describe a young man as a *youth*, or it may be a symbol, as when we use *Cross* to mean 'Christianity'. *Pen* is derived from Latin *penna*, meaning 'feather'. Originally applied to a quill pen, it was applied to pens of other kinds which replaced the quill. *Pencil* (Latin penicillus) originally meant a fine painter's brush. It was transferred to other marking instruments, some of which contained lead, and the term *lead pencil* remained in use when lead had been replaced by graphite. Another example of transference is *handkerchief.* A small piece of cloth to cover the head was in French called a *couvre-chef*, which gave us *kerchief*, a small piece of cloth used for any purpose. *Handkerchief* and *pocket handkerchief* represent later attempts to restrict its meaning.

Like metaphors, examples of metonymy fade and their origin is forgotten. OE *hlēor* 'cheek' survives in *leer*, to denote a particular expression of the face, sly and malignant. We are conscious of metonymy when we use *tongue* for 'language', but not as a rule in the word *language* itself, which is ultimately derived, with the addition of a suffix, from Latin *lingua* 'tongue'.

The name of the young of a species has often come to be used to denote the species as a whole. Thus *rabbit* has replaced *coney* in general use, and *pig* and *bird* have replaced *swine* and *fowl*. When the animal is used for food, commercial influences encourage the change, since the young animal is generally more palatable. Thus *chicken* and *lamb* are replacing *hen* and *mutton*, in spite of what one hopes will be a passing vogue for *sheepmeat* to denote both mutton and lamb.

A figure of speech which is found in both literature and everyday life is hyperbole, which is the use of exaggeration for the purpose of emphasis rather than deception, as when an oriental flatterer assures his sovereign that he will live for a thousand years and have fifty tall sons and fifty beautiful daughters, or when Gibbon says 'a thousand swords were plunged at once into the bosom of the unfortunate Probus'.[5] That the motive is rhetorical rather than an attempt to deceive is generally made clear by the extent of the exaggeration.

Excessive use of hyperbole has the effect of weakening the words that are so used. The original meaning of *astonished* was 'thunderstruck' and that of *surprised* was 'captured', but both words have now been weakened in meaning. Words expressing affirmation or negation are particularly liable to be used with needless emphasis and, thus weakened, they need constant reinforcement. *Yes* becomes *quite so*, *indeed*, *the answer is dead yes* or *I certainly will*, and *no* becomes *not possibly* or *no way*, just as in French negation is expressed by *ne pas* or *ne point*. There is a tendency to tone down disagreement. The classic example of the yes-man's 'no' is Evelyn Waugh's 'Up to a point, Lord Copper' (*Scoop* (1933) ch. 1), but almost every day we can hear *not really*, *hardly* and *scarcely* with the same meaning. Titles of honour, except those like *duke* and *lord* which can be clearly defined, tend to sink in the scale as a result of enlargement of the group to whom they are applied. To avoid giving offence most people act on the principle that if you are in doubt, you give them the title. We thus get *Esq*, originally a title of rank, and *Mr*, ultimately from Latin *magister* 'master', used for any male person. *Miss* and *Mrs* are used to indicate sex or marital status rather than authority. *Squire* has become a substandard term of address to a stranger on the offensive assumption that he will be flattered by the title.

We are all guilty of hyperbole at times, but many people think that one of the characteristics of English speech is a fondness for understatement, which arises from a desire to avoid hyperbole. George Mikes, by birth a Hungarian, was impressed by this characteristic:

> It is easy to be rude on the Continent. You just shout and call people names of a zoological character. . . . In England rudeness has quite a different technique. If somebody tells you an obviously untrue story, on the Continent you would remark 'You are a liar, Sir, and a rather dirty one at that'. In England you just say 'Oh, is that so?' Or 'That's rather an unusual story, isn't it?'
>
> When some years ago, knowing ten words of English and using them all wrong, I applied for a translator's job, my would-be employer (or would-not-be employer) softly remarked: 'I am afraid your English is somewhat unorthodox'. This translated into any continental language would mean: EMPLOYER (to the commissionaire): 'Jean, kick this gentleman down the steps!' . . . Terribly rude

> expressions (if pronounced grimly) are: 'I am afraid that . . .' 'unless . . .' 'nevertheless . . .' 'How queer . . .' and 'I am sorry, but . . .'[6]

Understatement is especially common in colloquial speech and slang. Money is described disparagingly as ***dough*** or ***brass*** or, in Victorian times, *tin*, for which the twentieth-century equivalent is perhaps *moolah*. The language of affection is rich in terms of disparagement, used ironically or from a desire to conceal deep feeling, as in Othello's 'excellent wretch' (*Othello*, III.3.90) or Pepys's 'my wife, poor wretch'.

The term 'irony' is used in many different senses. There are many legitimate meanings of 'ironically' as well as the common journalistic use of the word in the senses 'by a curious coincidence' or 'oddly enough', to which Philip Howard calls attention.[7] Two meanings of *irony* are important in connexion with the relation between language and literature. The simplest meaning is that defined by *COD* as 'expression of one's meaning by language of opposite or different tendency, especially simulated adoption of another's point of view or laudatory tone for purpose of ridicule'. This is the sort of irony that finds expression in substandard use in everyday life in such remarks as 'Charming!' used as an expression of disgust or 'You're a fine fellow' addressed to somebody who isn't or, in a worn-down form, in such phrases as 'That's all very well'. In literature it is another kind of irony that is important. This is defined by *COD* as 'use of language that has an inner meaning for a privileged audience and an outer meaning for the person addressed or concerned (occasionally including speaker)'. The existence of two points of view, one of which is better informed than the other, is an essential characteristic of this kind of irony. As a rule the speaker or writer is to be included among those with the better informed point of view, but occasionally he is not, as when someone telling a story arouses unexpected laughter by revealing that he himself is unaware of the full significance of what he says. When a similar situation arises in a literary work, the reader is always uncertain whether the author is indulging in a joke against himself.

Geoffrey Leech points out[8] that linguistic irony does not so much presuppose a double audience as a double response from the same audience. Irony loses its point unless the reader is conscious of both the literal and the implied meaning. There are many instances in literature, such as Swift's *Modest Proposal for preventing the Children of the Poor People from being a Burthen to their Parents* (1729), of a writer being so successful in maintaining a dead-pan seriousness that some of his readers fail to detect his use of irony. A cautious author avoids this danger by dropping the irony, sometimes with startling suddenness, before he leaves the subject. This is the course followed by Max Beerbohm in his essay 'Arise, Sir —— ——!' After writing some pages in ironical praise of 'Mr Flimflam, the popular novelist', he concludes his essay with the words:

> For my own part, I should like him to have a life-peerage. We have our Law-Lords – why not our Novel-Lords? It matters not what title he receive, so it be one which will perish, like his twaddle, with him.[9]

Another example of the dangers of irony occurs in *Martin Chuzzlewit*. Dickens found that one of his heavily ironical passages about Mr Pecksniff had been misunderstood, and he therefore added a footnote as a warning to other readers: 'The most credulous reader will scarcely believe that Mr Pecksniff's reasoning was once set upon as the Author's!!' (ch. 20).

Most books that were written more than two or three centuries ago contain some words that are no longer in general use, but there are some which contain words which were already archaic when the books were written. To detect such archaisms can be a difficult task for a reader of today, because he may know that words are now old-fashioned without knowing when they became so, and a dictionary gives little help. Even a large dictionary may give dated quotations without recording whether the writer who used a word thought of it as old-fashioned, new-fangled or commonplace. The best indication whether a word is an archaism is the impression that it makes on a reader familiar with the writings of the period in question. We are not concerned here with words that have become completely obsolete but with those that are half alive. The reader of today knows what they mean but he does not often use them himself. When such words are used in conversation, they are generally intended as a mild pleasantry, which quickly becomes tiresome. They include such words as *vale*, *damsel*, *steed*, *swain*, *morn*, *wight*, *fain*, *betimes*, *oft*, *ere* and *howbeit*. There are also poetic variants of everyday words, such as *'tis*, *e'er* and *spake*. Archaisms of meaning occur when words are used in senses which they once had though they have lost them today, as when *touching* is used to mean 'concerning'. Archaisms of accidence, like the past participle *holpen*, are common in the Authorised Version of the Bible, and in syntax we have such constructions as the use of *nothing* as an adverb ('a certain woman . . . was nothing bettered', Mark 5.25) or of *often* as an adjective ('thine often infirmities', 1 Timothy 5.23). There are also phrases which are now archaic, like 'And it came to pass'.

Archaisms often survive in poetry, but we sometimes find the converse process: poetic words can become prosaic with excessive use. Keats, in *Hyperion*, may have been the first to borrow *envisage* from the French, but it has now become part of the hackneyed language of the orator.

Spenser was especially fond of archaisms but he was also an innovator. Some of the older words that he revived, like *eke*, *whilom* and *wight*, are still thought of as archaisms, but others, like *astound* and *doom*, have passed into general use. Some of his innovations, like *askew*, *filch*, *flout* and *freak*, may have been borrowed from regional dialects,[10] but *blatant* was his own coinage. His archaisms aroused some hostile comment from his contemporaries, and Ben Jonson said that 'Spenser, in affecting the ancients, writ no language'.[11]

Another author who shared Spenser's fondness for words from dialects and the literature of the past was Walter Scott. By his example he changed the meaning of *glamour*, which was originally a north country variant of *grammar*. In an age when learning and magic were often confused, *glamour* came to mean 'a spell'. It is so used by Scott, but it has come to mean 'alluring charm'. Many of the archaisms revived by

Scott have failed to take a firm hold on the language. The words which he rescued from Lowland Scots dialects have fared better; they include such words as *gruesome* and *raid*. *Free-lance*, to denote a military adventurer, is now chiefly applied to journalists. *Fabliau*, denoting a medieval French tale in verse, was another word introduced by Scott and is in frequent use by historians of literature. *Smoulder* was current in the sixteenth century and then passed out of use until it was revived by Scott. *Stalwart*, a Scottish form of the archaic *stalworth*, was brought into English use by Scott.

Poets have sometimes made mistakes in their use of archaisms. Spenser often prefixed *a-* or *en-* to words which needed an extra syllable to improve the metre and in doing so he gave them an archaic flavour. The history of *derring-do* shows how several authors can share responsibility for the growth of an error. C. T. Onions, in *The Oxford Dictionary of English Etymology*, traces the history of the word from Chaucer's 'In dorrynge don that longeth to a knyght' i.e. 'In daring to do what appertains to a knight' (*Troilus and Criseyde*, V.837). The phrase was used as a noun by Lydgate, and Spenser glossed 'In derring doe' by 'In manhoode and cheualrie' (*Shepherd's Calendar*, October). Its widespread currency in the sense 'deeds of daring' is due to Scott's use of 'deeds of such derring-do' in chapter 29 of *Ivanhoe*. Another mistake was made independently by Chatterton and Browning, who were misled by the spelling of *slughorn* to suppose that it was a kind of trumpet, and we get the conclusion of one of Browning's best-known poems:

> Dauntless the slug-horn to my lips I set,
>   And blew 'Childe Roland to the Dark Tower came'.

Slughorn is an early form of *slogan*, which originally meant 'battle-cry', a loan-word from Gaelic *sluaghghairm*. *Iwis*, an adverb meaning 'certainly' (OE *gewis*), has often been mistaken for the first personal pronoun followed by a verb which was taken to mean 'know'. The mistake was encouraged by the existence of *wiste* as the preterite of *wot* 'I know'; the creation of a present tense *wis* from a preterite *wiste* is an example of back-formation.

In everyday conversation repetition is very common but it is not generally accounted a virtue. In conversation it is uncontrolled and is usually the result of clumsiness or incompetence or a conviction that what we have just said has not met with a reception suited to its importance; it is therefore necessary to say it again to make sure that our hearers have understood the point that we are making. In literature repetition of various kinds plays an important part, whether it be the repetition of initial or final sounds, as in alliteration and rhyme, the use of a refrain, or the more subtle variation on a theme similar to that which occurs in music. Similarly ambiguity, which we generally try to avoid in everyday life, unless we are addicted to making two-edged remarks, can be an important element in literature. The word as 'a general term for all kinds of secondary meaning' has been defined by Winifred Nowottny:

> The term 'ambiguity' now has a wide currency as a means of referring to diverse ways in which the language of poetry exhibits a charge of multiple implications and fits itself to contain within the form of discourse aspects of human experience whose difference or distance from one another might seem such as not easily to permit their coherent assembly in linguistic form.[12]

In literary criticism the term 'ambiguity' is used to call attention to the many-sidedness of language. Its linguistic basis is polysemy. As a result of the changes that have taken place in the meanings of words, creating new meanings without abolishing the old, most words in general use have many different meanings, and we have learnt to take them in our stride. These different meanings provide the poet with his opportunity. The number of opportunities that he can use is much smaller than the number theoretically possible because the context in which a word is used will generally rule out most of the meanings which are included in a dictionary.

Literary allusions and quotations are largely a matter of fashion. They provide evidence that writer and reader share a common culture, which serves as a kind of shorthand. The writer assumes that the reader is familiar with the quoted work, and a brief allusion saves him the time that would be taken by a detailed exposition of a subject that has already been dealt with by a master, just as a chess expert, writing for other experts, can refer to familiar end-games without working out the details. There are fashions in the use of quotations from foreign languages. In the eighteenth century a parliamentary orator could create a favourable impression by quoting Latin or, better still, Greek; today he would be accused of showing off. In the nineteenth century a few scraps of French were thought to lend tone to novels of fashionable society, like *The Lady Flabella* (3 vols), much enjoyed by Mrs Wititterley (*Nicholas Nickleby*, ch. 28).

Many phrases have passed into the everyday language from the plays of Shakespeare. Some of them are still thought of as quotations, though many of those who use them would be hard put to it to say exactly where they came from. Such phrases are 'the lady doth protest too much', 'to make assurance doubly sure', 'single blessedness', 'to smell to heaven', 'metal more attractive', 'every inch a king' and 'the windy side o' the law'. Others are homely phrases which have become semi-proverbial, like 'bag and baggage', 'eaten me out of house and home', 'to suit the action to the word', 'pride of place', 'a foregone conclusion', and 'salad days'. Such phrases are not generally thought of as quotations and those who use them feel no compulsion to preserve the exact words of the original; they will modify the wording to suit the needs of the moment. More important, they will change the meaning. It has often been pointed out that when Hamlet said that the firing of a cannon when the king drank a toast was a custom more honoured in the breach than the observance, he meant that it was a bad custom, whose abandonment would bring honour to the Danes. When the passage is quoted today, however, the meaning given to it is usually that the custom is more often broken that observed.

Excessive quotation is a vice of young and well-read writers. It is a vice because it makes for dull reading to be constantly referred to some authority for statements so commonplace that the reader would be willing to accept them as the author's own. But it is a vice that springs from the virtues of modesty and honesty. The author may just be showing off the extent of his own reading, but more often he is so lacking in self-confidence and so ready to acknowledge the merit of others that he quotes an authority for ideas that might have occurred to anyone and that he himself could have expressed just as effectively. Whatever his motives, he would be wise to avoid quotation unless the idea quoted is important or its expression felicitous.

Various devices are used to avoid the dullness of straightforward quotation. One of them is deliberate misquotation. By changing one word of a familiar quotation or proverb a writer coins a new epigram with an entirely different meaning, which acquires an added point for some of his readers by its echo of a familiar quotation. He may, for example, say that immigration is the sincerest form of flattery, confident that most of his readers will be familiar with a somewhat similar comment about imitation. A woman expressed her distaste for middle-aged bachelors by saying that a bachelor is too ready to assume that he is a thing of beauty and a boy for ever. The words of the original can sometimes be kept unchanged, but a word may be identified wrongly or used in a sense that both writer and reader know is not that intended by the author. John Wain, later to become Professor of Poetry at Oxford, prefaced his novel *Hurry On Down* (1953) with a quotation from Wordsworth's *A Poet's Epitaph* used in a sense of which its author would certainly have disapproved:

> A Moralist perchance appears;
> Led, Heaven knows how! to this poor sod.

A speaker congratulating a local authority on the generosity of its grants to students, said that his audience could feel that, like St Paul, they were citizens of no mean city.

Misquotations that are not deliberate are a different matter. We are today so ready to assume that usage is all that matters that we are perhaps too tolerant of common misquotations, but it is reasonable to make a distinction between quotation from a known source and the adoption of a word from the common vocabulary, where usage plays a more important part. The best justification of a quotation is that the author quoted has expressed an idea felicitously. If we are sufficiently impressed by his apt language to quote his words, the least that we can do is to quote them accurately, no matter how many other people have misquoted them, especially if the misquotation is demonstrably inferior to the original. The man who talks about gilding the lily not only has a bad memory but is insensitive to the careful use of words. The misquotation telescopes 'to gild refined gold, to paint the lily . . . Is wasteful and ridiculous excess' (*King John*, IV.2.11). To gild gold is obviously wasteful whereas to gild a lily is less obviously so.

A writer's problem is to know how far he can assume that he and his readers have a similar background. If they have, he can achieve lightness of touch by abstaining from explanations, as in the short story that I can quote in full from a school magazine: ' "Hurrah!" said the foremost lemming. "We're winning" '. The story loses much of its appeal if the narrator has to labour his point by explaining what a lemming is.

One device for lessening the dullness of quotations is the concealed quotation, about which opinions differ. Readers familiar with the quotation derive satisfaction from recognising it, but those who are less familiar feel that they are eavesdropping at a family party or that the author is expressing himself strangely, according to the extent of their partial recognition. Quotations that are likely to be treated in this way are those that are so familiar that they have passed into the idiom of everyday speech, as many proverbs have done. Such references can be regarded as allusions rather than quotations.

In the history of literature there are periods of conformity, like the eighteenth century in England, and periods of experiment, like the present day, when writing on well-established lines is not highly regarded. There are recurrent periods of similarity. The eighteenth century, like the Anglo-Saxon period, was a time when poetic diction flourished; the metaphysical poets of the seventeenth century, like the poets of today, were willing to experiment.

Some fashions last for a long time. One practice, followed in Anglo-Saxon times and surviving in legal documents today, is the linking together of two near-synonyms, like *idleness* and *sloth*. The mannerism was common in Middle English, and Caxton was fond of it. It often happens that one word of the pair is native and the other foreign, and it is sometimes said that the practice grew up when there were many speakers of French living in England, and in such a pair one word could serve as a gloss on the other. However, this cannot have been more than a contributory cause since, as McKnight points out,[13] the use of such pairs is even more common in Caxton's French sources than it is in Caxton, and there are many pairs in which both words are native or both foreign. When the two words are linked by 'that is' rather than 'and', as in 'charite þet is lufe', we may regard the second word as a gloss, and there is a parallel in English at the present day when, during a period of transition from Fahrenheit to centigrade measurement of temperature, BBC weather reports often record the temperature by both scales.

The linking of synonyms is especially common in the Book of Common Prayer, where we find pairs like 'sin and wickedness', 'assemble and meet together' and 'requisite and necessary'. Stella Brook defends the practice:

> The traditional English habit of using two words to express one idea can sometimes bring out the etymological sense of a loan-word which has now developed a specialised sense. One clear example can be seen in the Exhortation preceding the General Confession in The Communion: 'Ye that . . . are in love and charity with your neighbours'; one might also instance the doubling of 'regenerate and born anew' in the opening Exhortation of Publick Baptism. Because the etymological sense of *charity* and *regenerate* has now been largely lost, it is no longer easy to recognise that these two phrases do in fact illustrate simply a characteristic English means of stylistic amplification. This particular kind of word doubling, which involves the coupling of a word of native origin and

> a word of Latin origin, is a form of stylistic play which naturally has no counterpart in a language free from loan-words, such as Latin.[14]

The use of the device in legal documents has been defended by Sir Ernest Gowers on the grounds that the draftsman 'must limit by definition words with a penumbra dangerously large, and amplify with a string of near-synonyms words with a penumbra dangerously small'.[15]

A more short-lived fashion, which flourished in the sixteenth century, was euphuism, which delighted in antithesis and balance, alliteration and far-fetched similes drawn from 'unnatural natural history'. Another fashion which flourished at about the same time was a fondness for long and unfamiliar words of Latin origin, which became known as 'inkhorn terms'. The sixteenth century was an age when there were many important translations from foreign languages into English. When a translator could not find a good English equivalent of a Latin word, he would introduce the Latin word into his translation, sometimes in an Anglicised form. Today, when we have a rich English vocabulary, we should regard this as an unsatisfactory sort of translation, but in the sixteenth century the English vocabulary had fewer resources, and authors resorted to the introduction of foreign words in a deliberate attempt to enrich the language. The new words were not always welcome, but some of the words which aroused opposition have taken root in the language in spite of their length; such words are *alphabet*, *catastrophe*, *denunciation*, *emancipate*, *extravagant*, *penetrate* and *pernicious*.

Sixteenth-century prose-writers belonged to one of two opposing camps. Latinity was defended by Richard Mulcaster and Sir Thomas Elyot and attacked by Sir John Cheke, Thomas Chaloner and Sir Thomas Wilson. Both sides were guilty of excesses. It is possible to find passages of Elizabethan prose where Latin loans are so plentiful that the passage can hardly be recognised as English, and on the other side there are authors whose determination to avoid words of Latin origin leads them to indulge in native coinages that seem to us unnatural. Cheke translated Matthew's Gospel and where the AV has *lunatic* he has *mooned*; for *centurion* he has *hundreder*, for *proselyte* he has *freshman*, for *crucified* he has *crossed*, for *prophet* he has *foresayer* and for *parable* he has *byword*.[16] There was similar opposition to the excessive use of Italian loans. The choice of which inkhorn terms have survived and which have died, except as linguistic curiosities preserved in books on the history of language, often seems capricious. In *The Poetaster* Ben Jonson holds up to scorn a lot of inkhorn terms that his rival John Marston has used, but the list includes such words as *inflate*, *reciprocal*, *spurious* and *strenuous*, all of which are in common use today.

Punning was a common Elizabethan practice. Puns are not unknown today but in Elizabethan times they are used on serious occasions whereas today they are generally kept for trivial or light-hearted contexts.

The relaxation of manners that came with the Restoration is reflected in the language. J. A. Sheard points out[17] that, after the stern repression of the Commonwealth, the Restoration brought into use several words denoting scornful jesting and derision, and words that were first used or suddenly became popular at that time include *badinage*, *banter*, *burlesque*, *raillery*, *ridicule* and *travesty*.

In the early nineteenth century the term *romantic* came to be used to describe the scenes which were popular with the writers of early romances: old castles, mountains, forests and deserted wastes. Romantic writers were interested in wild nature and the emotions which it arouses, but they contemplated nature subjectively through a mist of literary associations. The antithesis between 'romantic' and 'classical' was developed on the Continent but it has been carried too far and applied too mechanically. There are both romantic and classical elements in most works of art. The Romantic Movement led to the revival of old words with new meanings to denote concepts popular with the Romantic poets. *Eerie* was used in Middle English in the sense 'fearful, timid'; it was first used in the sense 'fear-inspiring, gloomy' by Burns in 1792. *Quaint* in Middle English meant 'skilled, ingenious' and it was sometimes used with a pejorative sense 'cunning, crafty'; it acquired its present sense 'attractively unusual, old-fashioned' towards the end of the eighteenth century and Scott was one of the first to use the word in this sense. *Weird*, originally a noun meaning 'fate', was used in

Macbeth in the phrase 'the Weird Sisters'; it was revived by Shelley in the sense 'uncanny, unearthly'.

In the later nineteenth century there were many fashions, some of them short-lived. One of them is the polysyllabic humour which is common in the novels of Dickens and George Eliot. Literary devices remain in pockets when they have ceased to be fashionable, and polysyllabic humour, which is no longer highly regarded in literature, remains as a feature of the popular television show *The Good Old Days*, where each polysyllabic word used by the master of ceremonies is greeted with applause or friendly groans by the audience, which has learnt to expect it.

CHAPTER EIGHT

Language and Religion

In many civilisations there has been a tendency for a special form of language to develop for religious use. It is sometimes an entirely different language from that used in everyday life, as in those churches which use Latin in religious services, or it may be one register of the vernacular. In recent years there have been many attempts to lessen the divergence between the language of religion and that of everyday life. Instances of this tendency are the replacement of Latin by English in services in the Roman Catholic Church, the proposals for the revision of the Anglican Book of Common Prayer and the numerous new translations of the Bible into English that have appeared in recent years.

Religious language is of many different kinds. The most obvious division is that between spoken and written language, between the liturgical language of church services and the language used in translations of the Bible. David Crystal and Derek Davy point out[1] that the language of sermons has more in common stylistically with other varieties of public speaking than with liturgical language. The language of biblical translations has developed a style of its own, since such translations are often read aloud and constraints are imposed by the knowledge that they are translations. The author of the English text has to remember that his primary duty is to render the sense of the original rather than to create haunting cadences. The author of liturgies is better able to break free from these constraints. Stella Brook has emphasised the importance of taking advantage of this freedom:

> If English is to be used as the actual liturgical language, and not merely to provide a 'crib' to accompany a Latin liturgy, then respect for English idiom must be a necessary

> constituent of English liturgical style. The purely aural effects appropriate to liturgical writing – dignity, sonority, balance – must necessarily be required from any language used for public worship; it does not follow that only one means, the means natural to Latin, can achieve these effects.[2]

Another influence on the style of the liturgy is the tradition of devotional writing, where words have acquired special meanings. Liturgical language must be easily spoken aloud; words with heavy groups of consonants are unsuitable. It is necessary to pay attention to the changing views of congregations on the appropriateness to religious use of particular linguistic features. Fifty years ago a parson who addressed God as 'you' was liable to distract the attention of his congregation from his subject-matter to a comparatively unimportant feature of linguistic usage, whereas today the usage is becoming accepted. Modern attempts to make liturgical language approach more closely the language of everyday life have led to a reduction in the number of archaisms, a willingness to paraphrase theological terms and an avoidance of long and complicated sentences. The movement towards modernisation can go too far; most people prefer religious language to continue to be formal and dignified. Clergymen who use a colloquial style in order to be 'with it' may attract younger age-groups but are likely to arouse the disapproval or derision of older church-goers. There are differences between the liturgical language of different denominations. Nonconformists make less use of liturgical language than Anglicans but greater use of extempore prayers. They are more afraid of brevity than Anglicans and in their public prayers they often draw upon the language of hymns, incorporating many quotations, part-quotations and paraphrases.

The language of religion includes the technical terms of theology, such as *incarnate*, *grace*, *redemption* and *purgatory*. There are also phrases like 'works of supererogation', formulas like 'world without end' and 'this day and always' and figurative phrases like 'the lamb of God'. Some words are found also in other contexts but are especially common in religious use; such words are *obdurate*, *praise*, *glorify*, *exalt* and *remembrance*. A number of everyday words, like *shepherd*, *unclean*, *the world* and *the flesh*, have acquired a religious sense in addition to their everyday meanings. The words which cause most trouble are those which have a quite precise theological sense which is unknown to many people who are familiar with the words in more general contexts. James Hogg, the Ettrick Shepherd, published a book in 1824 which *DNB* describes as 'weighted at first with the repelling title *Confessions of a Justified Sinner*'; it was later called *Confessions of a Fanatic*. The original title is not so much repelling as technical. Hogg is using *justified* in the theological sense, recorded from the fourteenth century, 'declared free from the penalty of sin on the ground of Christ's righteousness, or made inherently righteous by the infusion of grace' (*OED* s.v. Justify 4). Another theological term which can be misleading is *particular* as used in the name of the sect the Particular Baptists. These are 'Baptists holding the Calvinistic doctrines of particular election and particular redemption, i.e. the Divine election and redemption of some, not all, of the human race' (*OED* s.v. Particular 2 d). Another sect is that of the Peculiar People, also called the Plumstead Peculiars, a religious sect founded in 1838, most of whose adherents live in or near London. They have no preachers or creeds but rely wholly on prayer for the cure of disease and reject medical aid (*OED* s.v. Peculiar 6 b).

It has often been pointed out that a large part of our supposed debt to the Authorised Version of the Bible of 1611 is in fact a debt to its predecessors, but it is not always realised how numerous these were; A. C. Partridge notes that more than fifty had been made by 1611.[3] Bernard Groom writes:

> The Authorized Version is the work not of an age but of many centuries; and its authority as an English classic is due largely to its preservation of the traditions of our language.[4]

The position of the Authorised Version in the tradition of English biblical translations is summed up by Sir Frederic

Kenyon:

> The translation which still holds the field and which to all except a small minority *is* the Bible, is that which we know as the Authorised Version, produced in 1611 by a committee appointed by James I. This was based on the translation of Tyndale (New Testament 1525, Pentateuch 1530, historical books posthumously in 1537), completed by Coverdale (1535, revised in Great Bible, 1539–41), and revised by King James's revisers with the help of the Geneva Bible (1560) and the Roman Catholic Rheims and Douai Bible (N.T. 1582, O.T. 1609). Its main character was indelibly imprinted on it by Tyndale and Coverdale, and it is a pre-eminent example of the dignified and expressive prose which is the special characteristic of Tudor translations.[5]

The contributions of Tyndale to the religious language still current today have more than once been pointed out by writers on the English language.[6] Bernard Groom points out that to Tyndale we owe the word *elder* as a literal equivalent of the Greek word previously rendered as 'priest' and the use of *congregation* in preference to *church*. The modern senses of *godly*, *ungodly*, *godless* and *godliness* are first found in Tyndale. *Weakling* was apparently suggested to him by Luther's *weichling*. The petition in the Lord's Prayer 'Forgive us our trespasses' is from the Book of Common Prayer and J. A. Sheard points out that it is ultimately from Tyndale, whereas the AV has 'debts'. Tyndale has also given us *peacemaker*, *long-suffering*, *stumbling-block* and *scapegoat*. Two familiar words go back to these early translators: from Tyndale we have *broken-hearted* and from Coverdale *kind-hearted*.

In view of its debt to earlier translations, it may seem misguided to concentrate attention on the Authorised Version in discussing the influence of biblical English on the language of everyday life but, whatever its sources, the AV is the version that most Englishmen have used from the date of its publication until that of the Revised Version of 1881, and even today the AV still maintains its hold on many speakers of English.[7]

The influence of biblical translations has been exerted both directly and indirectly. Much of their direct influence has been on men and women who read little else besides the Bible; their indirect influence has been exerted through writers like Ruskin who, from choice or parental pressure, in their childhood read portions of the Bible every day. A great variety of styles is to be found in the Bible. The most common style is that of straightforward narrative, but quite different styles are used in the Psalms, the poetical books such as Job and The Song of Songs, the Wisdom Books such as Proverbs and Ecclesiastes, and the exhortations of Paul. Certain characteristics are to be found, however, in all parts of the Authorised Version: a love of balance and antithesis and a carefully controlled rhythm.

Some words are familiar today largely because of their occurrence in the Bible. *Riotous* has diverged in meaning from *riot* because 'riotous living' is mentioned in Luke 15.13 in the parable of the prodigal son, where the context shows that *riotous* has the meaning 'extravagant, profligate'. *Ghost* is used in everyday life in the sense 'apparition', but it is also used in biblical senses, two of which are seen in the phrases 'the Holy Ghost' and 'to give up the ghost'. It means the spirit or immaterial part of a person, as distinct from the body. *Magnify* in the sense of rendering praise to God has become established in liturgical use and is therefore generally understood by church-goers, though it is archaic in general use. It is kept in many modern translations of the Bible. *Backbiting* 'slander' and *backsliding* 'faithlessness' have passed into everyday language from their biblical use.

Some words and phrases which are often thought of as biblical were coined many years after the date of the Authorised Version. *The hereafter* in the sense 'the life after death' is not used in the Bible as a noun; the earliest use of the word in this sense is in 1702, and it was popularised by John Wesley's frequent use of the word. *The faithful*, widely used today as a plural noun meaning 'true believers', is recorded from the late sixteenth century.

Some words which might otherwise have become obsolete keep a sort of half-life as a result of their occurrence in the Bible in passages that are often quoted. Such a word is *dayspring* 'daybreak, dawn', a poetic word based on the metaphor that dawn is the spring of the day; it is used in Luke 1.78 'whereby the dayspring from on high hath visited us'. *Ark* is used today chiefly with reference to Noah's Ark or the Ark of the Covenant, but it was once a common English noun meaning 'box'. It forms the first element of the surname *Arkwright*.

The most obvious difficulties which the language of the AV presents to a reader of today are those caused by words which to most readers are completely unfamiliar, such as *amerce* 'to fine', *latchet* 'shoe-lace', *leasing* 'falsehood' or *ouches* 'settings for jewels'. Unfamiliar words may be even more difficult if they happen to resemble familiar words of quite different origin, but the context generally provides a hint to guard against a mistaken identification, as in *to ear* 'to plough' and *reins* 'kidneys'.

A large and important group of words consists of those which survive in common use but which are used in the AV in senses now obsolete or archaic. Examples are *chargeable* 'burdensome', *doctor* 'teacher', *exceeding* 'very', *like* 'to please', *quick* 'alive', *target* 'light shield', *want* 'to lack', *without* 'outside'. *After* as a preposition often has the archaic sense 'according to'; as an adverb it means 'afterwards'. *Mess* is used in the AV in the sense 'a portion of food', a meaning close to that found in MnE *officers' mess*; the well-known phrase 'a mess of pottage' does not occur in the AV account of Esau's sale of his birthright (Genesis 25.29–34). The verb *seethe*, its past tense *sod* and its past participle *sodden* are all used in the AV in senses now obsolete. *Seethe* is a transitive verb meaning 'to cook food by boiling'; when Jacob 'sod pottage' (Genesis 25.29) he was boiling it. *Secure* in AV denotes a state of mind that is confident and free from apprehension. Today it means more than feeling safe; it means being safe. The distinction makes sense of what would otherwise be a puzzling passage in Shakespeare: 'And you all know, security Is mortals' chiefest enemy' (*Macbeth*, III.5.31). In Rome at the time of Christ a *publican* was a man who leased the right to collect taxes in a particular district; he paid a fixed sum and was allowed to keep any excess that he collected. Such men were naturally unpopular, and hence *publican* is used in AV in a pejorative sense; later translations read 'tax-collector'. *Tale* in AV has its present meaning 'narrative' in *talebearer*, but it also has the sense 'the complete number', as in the tale of bricks which Pharaoh required daily from the people of Israel (Exodus 5.8), and this may be the meaning in the well-known passage 'we spend our years as a tale that is told' (Psalm 90.9). Corresponding to the use of *tale* we have *tell* often used in the sense 'to count'. The idiom 'cannot tell', meaning 'do not know' occurs frequently in the AV; modern translations replace it by 'do not know'. The noun *vanity* in the sense 'undue self-esteem' is as old as the fourteenth century, but the adjective *vain* is not found in the sense 'conceited' until the end of the seventeenth. In AV *vain* always has its older meaning 'worthless, futile', and *vanity* means 'futility'. Down to the seventeenth century *to worship* meant to show due honour to human beings as well as to God, and this meaning is familiar today in the marriage service: 'With my body I thee worship'.

In the period that has elapsed since the production of the AV there has been time for many changes of meaning to take place. It is natural, therefore, that many words are used in the AV with a meaning closer to the etymological sense than that current today. When we find a word used in an unusual way, the etymology and the context are often enough to give us the meaning. Examples are innumerable:

admiration is used to denote wonder or astonishment without any implication of praise; this sense is close to that of Latin *mirari* 'to wonder at'. In Revelation 17.6 the writer expresses 'great admiration' for the woman arrayed in scarlet 'drunken with the blood of the saints and with the blood of the martyrs of Jesus'.

allow in AV has the meaning 'praise, approve' (Latin *allaudare* 'to praise'), as when Paul says 'that which I do I allow not' (Romans 7.15).

amiable today denotes even-tempered friendliness and refers only to persons; in the AV it can apply to things and has the etymological sense 'lovable', as in 'How amiable are thy tabernacles, O Lord of hosts!' (Psalm 84.1).

comfort is often used in the AV in the modern sense 'soothe, console', but there are many occurrences which can best be understood by remembering its derivation from Latin *fortis* 'strong'. In later translations it is often replaced by *encourage*.

declare originally meant 'to make clear, explain'; now it means 'to make a formal public utterance'. When Pharaoh told Joseph about his dream, he said 'there was none that could declare it to me' (Genesis 41.24).

feebleminded is now used as a synonym of 'mentally

deficient'. The meaning in AV can best be arrived at by going back to the meanings of the two elements of the compound. It thus means 'fainthearted'.

footmen, too, can best be understood by ignoring the later semantic development of the word and looking at the meanings of the two elements. Footmen are foot-soldiers.

generation usually has its modern sense in AV, but there are important exceptions. In Matthew 1.1. it means 'genealogy' and in the famous expression 'generation of vipers' (Matthew 12.34) it means 'offspring' or 'brood'.

hardly means 'with difficulty', as in 'a rich man shall hardly enter into the Kingdom of God' (Matthew 19.23). The modern sense 'scarcely' is a later weakening.

person is from Latin *persona*, a mask worn by an actor. When the AV says that 'God is no respecter of persons' (Acts 10.34) it refers to the outward appearance or circumstances of men. The text means that God does not regard mere externals.

prevent in AV always has the sense 'go before, anticipate' (Latin *prae-* 'before' and *venire* 'to come'). When the psalmist says 'I prevented the dawning of the morning' (Psalms 119.147) he means 'I rose before dawn'.

whole is often used in the sense 'in good health, healthy', a meaning which seems natural when we remember that it is from OE *hāl* and that *heal* is from *hǣlan*, a derivative of this adjective.

Since metaphors form such an important element of our language, it is worth while to look at the religious use of metaphor. Dead and dying metaphors are at least as common in religious language as in any other variety. What makes such language difficult to understand is that any group of people will include some for whom the metaphors are dead, some for whom they are very much alive, and all the possible groups between these two extremes. Don Cupitt has put the problem clearly:

> But religious metaphors die with unreflective overuse. Words like redemption and grace go on being used, and in a sense people still know what they mean, but they are no longer closely tied to the concrete situations in which they

> originally arose. People, for example, do not tie grace to gratuity. And since religion, as a practical force, lives by metaphor, dead religious metaphors mean dead religion. It is for this reason, I suppose, that T. S. Eliot called the theologians who wrote the New English Bible unconscious atheists. They still knew the meanings of the old terms, but they did not write as men for whom religious metaphors were really alive.[8]

One of the most important kinds of metaphor found in the Bible is that which uses concrete terms to express abstract ideas. For example, *bowels* often denotes feelings or emotions, as we use *heart*. In the Song of Solomon 5.4 AV has 'my bowels were moved for him'. *Purge* is used more than thirty times in the AV, but never with reference to the purging of the bowels; it is always used metaphorically with the meaning 'cleanse, purify', and it often refers to a ceremonial ritual. *Carriage* in AV denotes what is carried rather than the act of carrying or a vehicle used for carrying. 'David left his carriage in the hand of the keeper of the carriage' (1 Samuel 17.22) means that David left his baggage with the man who was looking after the other baggage. *Eminence* in AV refers only to physical height and not to qualities, but *pre-eminence* does apply to human qualities. *Heaviness* occurs fourteen times in the AV but never in the sense of physical weight; it means 'sorrow, anxiety'. The adjective *heavy* is used of both grief and physical weight.

Many words no longer current can be identified because they survive as elements of compound words or because closely related words exist today. The reader with a knowledge of the history of the language is at an advantage here because the connexion between such pairs of words is not always obvious. For example, *neesing* (Job 41.18) is a variant of *sneezing*. *OED* says that *fnese* went out of use in the fifteenth century to be replaced by *nese*, with loss of the initial *f*, or *snese*, where the initial *f* had been misread as long *s*. *List* 'to please', as in 'The wind bloweth where it listeth' (John 3.8) survives in *listless* and is related to *lust*, which originally meant 'pleasure'. The meaning of the verb *wit* 'to know' can be guessed from that of the noun *wit*. When words found in AV occur today as elements of compounds or with affixes, they usually cause little trouble to a reader. *Prefer* today denotes an attitude of mind, but in AV it usually has the older sense of advancement or promotion, a sense found in MnE *preferment*. *Blain* 'blister' is archaic, but it is familiar in *chilblain*. *Stead* 'place' survives in *homestead*, *instead* and many place-names. *Froward* 'perverse' is a compound of the *fro* found in the phrase 'to and fro' (ON *frá*) and the *-ward* found in *toward*. *Minish* has contributed to the blend which has given *diminish*. *Divers* 'several' and *diverse* 'different' began to diverge about the end of the seventeenth century; *divers diseases* (Matthew 4.24) has the spelling of one variant and the meaning of the other. *Fat* is used for *vat* without the southern voicing of the initial consonant that has been preserved in the modern form. *Twain* is from the old masculine (OE *twēgen*), while *two* is from the feminine and neuter (OE *twā*). *OED* says that the use of *twain* in the AV and the marriage service has helped in its retention as an archaic and poetic synonym for *two*.

In many words the variation between the biblical and the modern form results from the loss of a prefix or suffix or the substitution of a different one. Examples are *afore* for *before*, *ambassage* for *embassy*, *astonied* for *astonished*, *ensample* for *example* and *fray* for *affray*. *Alway* is the older form of *always* without the adverbial *-s*; it is fairly common in the AV but it had already begun to be archaic and poetical. We are familiar with *endure* in the sense 'to last' but not with *dure*, except in the preposition *during*, which is derived from the verb; *dure* is found in AV (Matthew 13.21). *Entreat* occurs several times in the expression 'be entreated', which means 'be persuaded to grant the object of an entreaty'. It is also used as a synonym of *treat*: Julius courteously entreated Paul (Acts 27.3). *Fine* as a verb means 'refine', as in 'Surely there is a vein for the silver, and a place for gold where they fine it' (Job 28.1). *Gender* is used for *engender* with reference to the breeding of cattle in Leviticus 19.19. It is used in the sense 'give rise to' in 'Foolish and unlearned questions . . . do gender strifes' (2 Timothy 2.23). *Gin* is used for *engine*, which first meant 'ingenuity' then 'the products of ingenuity'. In the AV *gin* generally means a snare or trap. *Spoil* is used for *despoil*, *stablish* for *establish* and *ware* for *aware*. *Tire* is used for *attire*; as a noun it means 'ornament' and as a verb it means 'adorn'. It has nothing to do with the verb *tire* 'to grow weary'. *Disannul* is used in the sense 'annul' or 'cancel' (Galatians 3.17); it survives in modern dialects. *Remove* is used to mean 'move', both literally and figuratively, without the implication that the change of place is to be permanent.

There is similar variation in the use of suffixes. We often find that words derived from the same stem with different suffixes undergo divergent sense-development. *Attendance* is used in the AV to mean 'attention'; Paul urges Timothy to 'give attendance to reading, to exhortation, to doctrine' (1 Timothy 4.13). *Equal*, like Latin *aequus*, of which it is a derivative, is used in the AV to mean 'fair, just', a sense which we give today to *equitable*. 'Give unto your servants that which is just and equal' (Colossians 4.1) means 'Treat your servants justly and fairly'. There are in the AV several examples of the archaic practice of splitting up the preposition *toward* by inserting its object between the two elements of which it is composed, as in *to God-ward* and *to us-ward*.

Some rather long compound words have passed from the AV into general use. One of these is *longsuffering* 'patient endurance of provocation', also used as an adjective; in later translations it is replaced by *patience* or *forbearance*. *Thankworthy* can still be understood today, but the word is not so well established in the language as *praiseworthy* or *blameworthy*. *Stronghold* is a well-established compound, but the second element occurs by itself several times in AV with the same meaning, as in Judges 9.46. Some compounds have not taken root in the language. It is clear that *uncorruptness* (Titus 2.7) is equivalent to *incorruptibility*, but the meaning of *will-worship* (Colossians 2.23) is less obvious. *OED* defines it as 'worship according to one's own will or fancy, or imposed by human will, without divine authority'.

Some words are used in the Authorised Version in senses that are familiar to dialect speakers but no longer current in standard English. *Frame* is used in a passage often quoted to show the importance of acquiring correct pronunciation: 'and he said Sibboleth: for he could not frame to pronounce it right. Then they took him, and slew him.' (Judges 12.6). *Frame* is common in northern dialects in the sense 'to set about a task efficiently', and the same passage has given us *shibboleth* to denote a test-word but later used disparagingly to denote a doctrine that has been generally abandoned. *Inward* as an adjective in AV means 'intimate', but it is used twenty times in Exodus and Leviticus as a plural noun to denote the entrails of an animal offered in sacrifice. Later translations replace *inwards* by *entrails*. In the form *innards* it is common in dialects. The only meaning of *poll* as a noun in AV is 'the human head'. As a verb it means 'to cut off the hair of the head', as in the account of Absalom, who had a haircut once a year: 'he polled his head, for it was at every year's end that he polled it: because the hair was heavy on him' (2 Samuel 14.26). Both verb and noun are common in northern dialects with reference to haircuts. *Stuff* usually denotes various textile materials, but it is often used to mean 'movable property', as in modern dialects. *Besom*, a broom made of twigs tied round a stick, is found in the AV and is common in northern dialects.

In a sense all new translations of the Bible are revised versions, but the term Revised Version is generally accepted as the name of the translation of the New Testament published in 1881 and of the Old Testament published in 1884. It was produced as the result of a report submitted to the Convocation of Canterbury in May 1870. The revisers were empowered to co-opt eminent biblical scholars of any religious denomination. The directives for revision were to introduce as few changes as possible into the text of the Authorised Version and as far as possible to limit the expression of such changes to the language of the AV and earlier English versions. This directive meant that the language of the new text had to be limited to the vocabulary of Tudor and Jacobean authors, and the result has been described as a literary anachronism.

The influence of the Bible on our everyday language is hard to measure just because it is so great. A recent loan-word stands out in a passage of English prose because it is so different from its context, but if a foreign influence has thoroughly permeated a language, individual examples of the influence are no longer noticeable, because there is no contrast between the new word and the rest of the language.

C. S. Lewis has pointed out how great the unsuspected influence of biblical imagery may be:

> In imagery I suppose the influence to be very great, though I must frankly confess that I have not been able to invent a method of checking it. If English writers in elevated contexts tend to speak of corn and wine rather than of beef and beer and butter, of chariots rather than chargers, of rain rather than sunshine as a characteristic blessing, of sheep more often than cows and of the sword more often than either the pike or the gun, if bread rather than mutton or potatoes is their lofty synonym for food, if stone is more poetical than brick, trumpets than bugles, and purple and fine linen loftier than satin and velvet, I suspect that this is due to the Bible, but I have no rigorous proof. Nor, in this sphere, would it be easy to distinguish the Biblical influence from that generally Mediterranean and ancient influence which comes from the classics as well as the Bible. But I believe the Biblical influence is here very great.[9]

There is evidence of our reliance upon the text of the Bible in our use of the phrase 'chapter and verse' to denote the exact context of an allusion. The expression came into use at a time when it was assumed that any reference to authority would be to the Bible, but it is now widely used in secular contexts.

The influence of the Bible is more easily detected in phrases than in single words. When Bible-reading was the daily practice of large numbers of people, phrases of biblical origin were used freely, and some of them are in general use today because they have become proverbial. Such phrases are 'no respecter of persons', 'fear and trembling' and 'put new wine into old bottles'. Some biblical phrases are used satirically, such as 'loaves and fishes' and 'milk and honey', and others have become clichés, like 'filthy lucre' and 'my name is Legion'. There are homely expressions like 'heap coals of fire upon his head', 'at the last gasp' and 'all things to all men' as well as many that we recognise as religious or poetical without always knowing their exact source, such as 'he smote them hip and thigh', 'God is not mocked', 'the powers that be' and 'the fatted calf'.

Some biblical phrases have passed so completely into our

everyday language that many of those who use them are unaware of their biblical origin. By constant use they have lost much of the vigour that they once had. When we speak of grinding the faces of the poor we generally refer to less violent ill treatment, and when we say that we have escaped with the skin of our teeth, we lose sight of the vigour of the image. Many people think that images like casting pearls before swine or the leopard changing his spots are proverbial without realising that they are also biblical.

Some biblical quotations are so familiar that an author can deliberately misquote them, confident that his readers will recognise that he has completely changed the point of the original. It was said of Ibsen that he came not to call sinners but the righteous to repentance (cf. Matthew 9.13), and another writer, remembering Matthew 10.16, felt much better when he had said that the people with whom he disagreed were as harmless as serpents and as wise as doves. Some passages have been so often misquoted that the misquotation has become more familiar than the true reading. 'Pride goes before a fall' is a telescoping of 'Pride goeth before destruction and a haughty spirit before a fall' (Proverbs 16.18), and 'Spare the rod and spoil the child' is from Samuel Butler's 'Then spare the rod, and spill the child' (*Hudibras*, part II, canto 1, line 844), a modification of 'He that spareth his rod hateth his son' (Proverbs 13.24).

Many familiar phrases, such as 'for better for worse', 'the world, the flesh and the devil' and 'to have and to hold' are from the Book of Common Prayer. There are sometimes signs that a phrase in common use goes back to the version of the Psalms in the Book of Common Prayer rather than to the Authorised Version. When we say that the ungodly man flourishes like a green bay tree, we are relying on the Prayer Book version (Psalms 37.36); the AV speaks of the wicked man spreading himself like a green bay tree. The familiar phrase 'by the waters of Babylon' is from the Prayer Book version of Psalm 137; the AV has 'by the rivers of Babylon'.

Some phrases that have a biblical ring are really from secular sources. Such a phrase is 'God tempers the wind to the shorn lamb', which is ultimately from a French proverb, though the exact words are from Sterne's *A Sentimental Journey (Maria)*. Another is 'a man of light and leading', which is from Disraeli's *Sybil* (bk 5, ch. 1). It is natural that quotations from Bunyan should use the simple language that we expect to find in the Bible; it is in *The Pilgrim's Progress* that we find 'Sleep is sweet to the labouring man'.

Phrases from the Bible can change their meaning with the changes in our attitude to religion. To Coverdale, writing in 1535, 'a man of the world' means 'a worldy person'. To Fielding, writing in 1749, it is a term of commendation, meaning someone experienced in the ways of the world. It has lost its associations of religious disapproval. There have been similar fluctuations in the meaning and status of *enthusiasm*. The Puritans used this word in its literal sense of 'inspiration'. To their opponents it meant self-delusion and misdirected religious emotion, and in the eighteenth century it is usually a term of abuse. It has now lost this pejorative sense but, in losing it, it has become secularised. The present meaning 'rapturous intensity of feeling' is found as early as 1716. So too *visionary*, which originally meant 'accustomed to see visions', is used by Swift in 1727 in the sense 'given to fanciful and unpractical views' (*OED* s.v. Visionary A.1).

In plays and novels from the seventeenth century onwards the introduction of characters whose language betrays a strong biblical influence became a popular feature. The language that was associated with Methodists in the eighteenth century is described by Richard Graves in his account of Geoffrey Wildgoose:

> though he had really a classical taste; and, on common subjects, an elegance of expression; yet, by confining himself so long to the puritanical writings above-mentioned, and those of the Methodists, he had strongly imbibed their manner: and his language on religious topics abounded with that strange jargon of those pious people, which chiefly consists in applying the quaint Hebraisms of the Old Testament; and the peculiar expressions of the primitive apostles to their own situations, and every trifling occurrence of modern life.[10]

Characters who use such language in the affairs of ordinary life are usually unpleasant; Stiggins in *Pickwick Papers* and Chadband in *Bleak House* are familiar examples. But the habit is shared by an admirable character, Caleb Garth in *Middlemarch*, and George Eliot's comment on his use of biblical language is a good description of the influence exerted by the Bible without leading to direct quotation:

> '. . . The soul of man,' said Caleb, with the deep tone and grave shake of the head which always came when he used this phrase – 'the soul of man, when it gets fairly rotten, will bear you all sorts of poisonous toad-stools, and no eye can see whence came the seed thereof.'
>
> It was one of Caleb's quaintnesses, that in his difficulty of finding speech for his thought, he caught, as it were, snatches of diction which he associated with various points of view or states of mind; and whenever he had a feeling of awe, he was haunted by a sense of Biblical phraseology, though he could hardly have given a strict quotation. (ch. 40).

This is the approach to religious language which is revealed in Mr Sapsea's account of his proposal of marriage to Miss Brobity:

> When I made my proposal, she did me the honour to be so overshadowed by a species of Awe, as to be able to articulate only the two words, 'O Thou!' meaning myself . . . and, though encouraged to proceed, she never did proceed a word further (*Edwin Drood*, ch. 4).

Just as the language of poetry observes the same principles in the use of imagery as the language of everyday life, although it applies them more often and with greater freedom, so the language of religion must be based upon that of everyday life, using figures of speech more freely but with the same precautions against misuse and misunderstanding. A lecturer learns not to be too ready to ask a rhetorical question lest an over-zealous member of his audience should answer it, and a preacher has to be even more careful, because failure to recognise such a question may be concealed by his congregation's good behaviour. Only rarely is the failure shared by the preacher himself. A theological student was explaining to a college tutor how he would preach a sermon on the text 'How shall we escape if we neglect so great a salvation?' (Hebrews 2.3).

'Well, I should begin by explaining what is meant by so great a salvation.'

Murmurs of approval from the tutor.

'And then I should tell them how they can escape if they neglect it.'

The murmurs of approval abruptly ceased.

There are dangers in the use of a distinctive vocabularly on religious occasions; the chief is that it encourages people to think the religion has nothing to do with everyday life. A church-goer who had just listened to a sermon on the Ten Commandments was heard to mutter 'Well, I've never made a graven image'. Another danger is that the meaning of archaic language may not be understood. An extreme instance occurred when a visitor to a country church was moved by the clergyman's eloquence in appealing for funds to put a five-pound note on the collection plate. The clergyman in his turn was moved by this unexpected generosity to conclude the service with a prayer of thanks 'for this succour that has been sent to us'. Fortunately *succour* and *sucker* occur in different registers, and only the more irreverent members of the congregation professed to misunderstand the clergyman.

Religious language has its slang and class dialects. Most people know that a clerical collar is a *dog-collar*, and most Anglicans know that a High Churchman is a *spike*, though both terms are slang. In Scotland an episcopalian is known as a *piskie*. There are different terms to denote a man who is colloquially known as a parson. On formal occasions nonconformists describe him as a *minister*; Anglicans speak of a *clergyman*, a *priest* or a *clerk in holy orders*. He may be a *rector* or a *vicar*, according as the tithes formerly passed to the incumbent or to a chapter or religious house or layman.

Many of the names of festivals and seasons of the year had a religious origin, though the religion was sometimes older than Christianity. *Easter* is from OE *ēastre*, derived from the name of a goddess whose feast was celebrated at the vernal equinox; it was transferred to become the name of a Christian festival. *Christmas* is clearly Christian, but the older form *Yule* (OE *gēol*) was originally the name of a non-Christian feast lasting for twelve days. *Noel* is from OFr *noel* and is cognate with *natal*; it was applied especially to a Christmas carol, but the word *carol* itself was used from the thirteenth century to denote a ring-dance accompanied by song, and only in the sixteenth century did it come to be associated especially with Christmas. *Whitsun* is the result of misdivision. *White Sunday* was the name given to the seventh Sunday after Easter because of the custom of wearing white robes at the feast of Pentecost, to which it corresponded. *Shrove Tuesday*, the last day before Lent, and *Shrovetide*, the last three days, are cognate with the verb *to shrive* and refer to the practice of going to confession before Lent. *Ash Wednesday*, the first day of Lent, derives its name from the custom of sprinkling ashes on the heads of penitents. *Maundy Thursday*, the last Thursday before Easter, is from OFr *mandé*, from Latin *mandatum* 'commandment', an allusion to John 13.14, and *Palm Sunday*, the Sunday before Easter, celebrates Christ's entry into Jerusalem by processions in which palms are carried. *Lent* is an exception to the general tendency for religious terms to acquire a secular meaning. It is from OE *lencten* 'spring' and is cognate with the adjective *long*; it originally referred to the lengthening of days in spring. *Lady Day*, 25 March, is frequent in secular use as a quarter day, but it is so called because it is the Feast of the Annunciation. *Lammas* is 1 August. It was a feast observed in Anglo-Saxon England by the consecration of bread made from the first ripe corn. It is from OE *hlāfmæsse*, a compound of *loaf* and *mass*.

CHAPTER NINE

Reform

From the sixteenth century onwards there has been no lack of critics writing in praise or dispraise of the English language either in general or on points of detail which happened to interest them. Some of the critics have been well-known men of letters, and such writers may choose to exert an influence by example rather than precept. Swift was one of the most vigorous of the reformers of English, but he has probably exerted more influence by the straightforward simplicity of his own style than by his fulminations against changes that he disliked. If a writer wishes to make more specific criticisms, he can do so by writing essays on linguistic matters or by including digressions in books on other subjects. Readers of novels have learnt to be tolerant of such digressions. Another channel for criticism is provided by characters in novels or plays who comment, usually with scorn, on the language used by others. There is a less direct form of criticism taking the form of the allocation of language which the author thinks foolish to foolish characters without any comment. The linguistic eccentricities of Osric would be obvious enough even if Hamlet did not pour scorn on them, and Sir Andrew Aguecheek has affectations beside those which arouse the mockery of Sir Toby and Maria. All these kinds of criticism may be found in a single work. In *Northanger Abbey* Jane Austen allows herself a long digression in defence of novels in the course of which she attacks the coarse language of the *Spectator* (ch. 5), but her usual medium of criticism is Henry Tilney, with his mockery of Catherine's use of such words as *amazingly* and *nicest* (ch. 14), and both Isabella Thorpe and her brother are made to use language foolishly without comment from the author.

Linguistic criticism is common in the plays of Shakespeare. Polonius is both critic ('Mobled queen is good') and object of criticism ('More matter with less art'). The critics of language in Shakespeare are not only the characters who might be expected to be great readers. Doll Tearsheet says of the word *occupy* that it 'was an excellent good word before it was ill sorted' (*2 Henry IV*, II.4.159), and Hotspur criticises the language of 'metre ballad-mongers' (*1 Henry IV*, III.1.130) as well as the oaths appropriate to a comfit-maker's wife (III.1.253). There are abundant examples in the novels of Dickens. Mrs General in *Little Dorrit* is the most exacting ('Father is rather vulgar, my dear' bk II, ch. 5), but there are many others.[1]

The wide variety of interests and competence of fictional critics of language is matched by their counterparts in real life. The critics often show a complete ignorance of the principles of linguistic development, but their ignorance does not deprive their comments of value for those who are interested in the history of the language. Our earliest information about the changes which took place in early Modern English is often to be obtained from the protests of grammarians who reprehended the changes as mistakes, and Swift's complaints about new words, though often based on inadequate knowledge, tell us much about the colloquial language of his time.

The chief fault of uninformed criticism of language is a fondness for inventing new sins. The critic begins with an assumption that the use of one particular class of words is blameworthy and then produces examples which he claims to be instances of linguistic degeneracy. Categories which have come under fire both in the past and today include loan-words, words which contain elements from two or more different languages, monosyllabic words and words of American origin. The reply to all these attacks is not to deny the charges but to say that there is no earthly reason why such words should not be used and to point out that the categories under attack are so large that to expel them for the reasons given would be an intolerable impoverishment of the language.

Many of the comments on the English language have been collected[2] and it is interesting to see how the same subjects crop up again and again in the writings of eighteenth-century critics as well as in angry letters to the newspapers at the present day. What the critics chiefly dislike is change of any kind. This attitude leads to resistance to reform, but when the changes under attack become established, those who oppose them become reformers in their turn in their attempts to restore a linguistic golden age, real or imaginary, that they believe to have existed in the past.

In number 230 of the *Tatler* Swift complains of the 'continual corruption of the English tongue', of 'abbreviations and elisions, by which consonants of most obdurate sound are joined together, without one softening vowel to intervene'. He also complains of the shortening of polysyllabic words, producing forms like *phizz* and *incog*, and he describes monosyllables like *rep* and *mob* as 'the disgrace of our language'. He regards as vulgarisms new words like *bamboozle*, *banter* and *kidney* in the sense 'kind, disposition'. He disapproves of some young clergymen who 'in their sermons use all the modern terms of art, *sham*, *banter*, *mob*, *bubble*, *bully*, *cutting*, *shuffling* and *palming*'. It is not only short words that he dislikes; he protests also against polysyllabic words brought into common use by the war with France, such as *operations*, *preliminaries*, *ambassadors*, *pallisadoes*, *communication*, *circumvallation* and *battalions*.

Because of the vigour with which Swift attacked monosyllabic words, we tend to associate antipathy to their use with him, but he was not alone. Many writers on the English language during the eighteenth century were concerned about the growth in the number of monosyllabic words. Addison discussed them in some detail in the *Spectator* of 4 August 1711. He mentions the chief causes of the increase: the loss of *e* in the ending *-ed* of the preterite of weak verbs, the replacement of *-eth* by *-s* in the present indicative of verbs, the use of contracted forms like *shan't* and *won't*, and the curtailment of long words in familiar writing and conversation to give such words as *mob*, *rep* and *incog*. Addison's proposed remedy for these evils is one that we find again and again in the writings of reformers: these matters 'will never be decided till we have something like an Academy, that by the Best Authorities and Rules drawn from the Analogy of Languages shall settle all Controversies between Grammar and Idiom'.

Some of the hostility to monosyllables came from poets,

who felt that they clogged the smooth flow of verse and made it difficult to use dactyls and anapaests. Other objections were that they were slangy, over-emphatic and unlike Latin and Greek words, and that they made the English bark like dogs. Monosyllabic words had their defenders, who maintained that they gave strength and force to the language and that they were useful in the creation of compounds.[3] The controversy is one that does not trouble us much today because English is now so rich in words both long and short that it is an easy matter to achieve the mixture of long and short words that the reformers advocated, and most of us do it without conscious thought. Such a mixture is desirable because it enables a writer to make use of the full riches of the language, and we have grown used to it. As a *tour de force* a reviewer once wrote an article in a literary journal wholly in monosyllabic words until he reached the last two lines. I remember the sense of relief that I felt on reaching those lines after the sledgehammer blows of the monotonous succession of monosyllabic words.

Side by side with the attacks on monosyllabic words we find complaints about the excessive use of Latin and Greek loan-words, which were usually polysyllabic. Such attacks are common in the sixteenth century and continue into the next century. George Puttenham, in *The Arte of English Poesie* (1589), had suggested many compounds, made up from English or French elements, to replace the rhetorical terms, most of them of Greek origin, which so fascinated his contemporaries. For *zeugma* he suggested *single supply*, for *allegory*, *false semblant*, for *irony*, *dry mock*, and for *hyperbole*, *ouer-reacher*.[4] It is worth noting that these translations are not all self-explanatory. Dryden in his 'Dedication of the Æneis' (1697) defends his use of loan-words:

> 'Tis true, that, when I find an English word significant and sounding, I neither borrow from the Latin, nor any other language; but, when I want at home, I must seek abroad . . . We have enough in England to supply our necessity; but, if we will have things of magnificence and splendour, we must get them by commerce. Poetry requires

> ornament; and that is not to be had from our old Teuton monosyllables: therefore if I find any elegant word in a classic author, I propose it to be naturalized by using it myself; and, if the public approves of it, the bill passes. But every man cannot distinguish between pedantry and poetry: every man, therefore, is not fit to innovate. Upon the whole matter, a poet must first be certain that the word he would introduce is beautiful in the Latin, and is to consider, in the next place, whether it will agree with the English idiom: after this, he ought to take the opinion of judicious friends, such as are learned in both languages: and, lastly, since no man is infallible, let him use this licence very sparingly; for if too many foreign words are poured in upon us, it looks as if they were designed not to assist the natives, but to conquer them.[5]

Dryden shows moderation and most of what he says would be accepted today, though it would be difficult to apply some of his criteria, such as his requirement that the loan-word should be 'beautiful in the Latin'. What is a beautiful word? Probably the chief requirement would be ease of pronunciation, since many reformers complained of the heavy consonant groups in English words.

Both in the eighteenth century and at the present day critics have complained of the prevalence of vogue words. In both centuries the chief offenders seem to have been fashionable young women. Lord Chesterfield, in the *World* of 5 December 1754, complained of the popularity of *vast* and *vastly*:

> A fine woman (under this head I comprehend all fine gentlemen too, not knowing in truth where else to place them properly) is *vastly* obliged, or *vastly* offended, *vastly* glad or *vastly* sorry. Large objects are *vastly* great, small ones are *vastly* little; and I had lately the pleasure to hear a fine woman pronounce, by a happy metonymy, a very small gold snuff-box that was produced in company to be *vastly* pretty because it was *vastly* little.[6]

A. G. Macdonell, in *England Their England* (Macmillan, 1933), describes the twentieth-century counterpart of Lord Chesterfield's young lady:

> She was wearing a black frock which terminated in a sheaf of wispy, petal-shaped flounces, and was in no way disconcerted when, half-way through dinner, she deduced from a gleam of pale pink above her stocking that she had forgotten to put on any knickers. She had no topic of conversation and only one adjective at a time. At the moment the adjective was 'grisly' (ch. 6).

She reappears in a later chapter:

> Patience Ormerode was there, and Donald noticed two differences about her since they had sat down to dinner that evening at Ormerode Towers. Her universal adjective was now 'wan' instead of 'grisly', and she was wearing knickers (ch. 16).

Any group of reformers is liable to attract a lunatic fringe, and the fringe which surrounds reformers of language is larger than most. One of these extremists was John Pinkerton, who wrote under the pseudonym Robert Heron and published his *Letters of Literature* in 1785. In it he proposed some reforms of the English language and gave his reasons:

> The great secret of writing melodious English is surely to draw into view every possible word which may terminate in a vowel . . . I look upon the Greek as the most perfect language, both for strength and melody, that ever was known: now in Greek I have found that the vowel terminations of words taken as they run in any book, are equal to one third of the language. In English the vowel terminations amount but to one fourth of the language; it follows that we want vowel terminations for about 8000 words.[7]

Pinkerton goes on to suggest that the plural ending *-s* in English words should be replaced by *-a*, that in nouns ending in *-y* the *-y* should be replaced by *é* but that in adjectives it should be replaced by *-i*, and that nouns 'ending in harsh consonants' like *b* or *c* should take a final *-o*, as in *crabo* and *publico*. The interest of these proposals lies not in their importance, which is slight, or in their chances of acceptance, which are negligible, but as an illustration of the methods of the early reformers. They begin with an assumption that Greek and Latin are superior languages and that English would be improved if it were made to resemble them even in points of unimportant detail. They are not concerned about the cost of the reforms in time and trouble or about the negligible intrinsic value of the proposed reforms. They pay no attention to the history of the language or to the confusion that would result from the existence of a large body of older literature side by side with books written according to the proposed new patterns or to the effect of the reforms on the scansion of existing poetry. The reforms were put forward seriously, but they serve the purpose of Swift's account of his voyage to Laputa: they provide a parody of reforms which were being considered in the eighteenth century and which have their counterparts today.

The example of the French Academy led many English reformers to recommend the setting up of a similar body in England to decide which reforms were worth while and to give authority to the reforms of which it approved. One of the reformers was Daniel Defoe, who proposed that an academy should be set up by 'the King himself, if his Majesty thought fit'. The membership of this academy would present difficulties. Defoe wished to exclude clergymen, physicians and lawyers because 'their several professions do naturally and severally prescribe habits of speech to them peculiar to their practice and prejudicial to the study I speak of'. He was suspicious of academics:

> Into this Society should be admitted none but Persons Eminent for Learning, and yet none, or but very few, whose Business or Trade was Learning: For I may be allow'd, I suppose, to say, We have seen many great Scholars, meer Learned Men, and Graduates in the last

> Degree of Study, whose English has been far from Polite, full of Stiffness and Affectation, hard Words, and long unusual Coupling of Syllables and Sentences, which sound harsh and untuneable to the Ear, and shock the Reader both in Expression and Understanding.[8]

It is interesting to see that occupational dialects were already well established at the time of Defoe. The qualifications of the gentry would be equally under suspicion, for Defoe says of them that ''twere to be wished our gentry were so much lovers of learning that birth might always be joined with capacity'. The few men who satisfied Defoe's rigorous tests would have considerable powers, for

> no Author wou'd have the Impudence to Coin without their Authority . . . There shou'd be no more occasion to search for Derivations and Constructions, and 'twou'd be as criminal then to Coin Words, as Money.

Swift, too, advocated the setting up of an academy, which was to consist of 'such persons as are generally allowed to be best qualified for such a work'. This suggestion glides over one of the problems of an academy: how is this general agreement to be arrived at? The members of the academy 'will observe many gross improprieties which, however authorised by practice and grown familiar, ought to be discarded'. So much for usage. He then makes the proposal, which has been made many times but which most scholars today would agree to be wholly impracticable, that all change must cease:

> But what I have most at heart, is that some Method should be thought on for *Ascertaining* and *Fixing* our Language for ever, after such Alterations are made in it as shall be thought requisite. For I am of opinion, that it is better a Language should not be wholly perfect, than that it should be perpetually changing; and we must give over at one Time or other, or at length infallibly change for the worse.[9]

In the nineteenth century there was a revival of the controversy about loan-words. The most active of the reformers who sought to free the English language from its loan-words was William Barnes (1801–86), the Dorsetshire poet and friend of Thomas Hardy. He presented his case in an article published in the *Gentleman's Magazine* in 1832,[10] in which he denied that loan-words are more elegant or meaningful than native words and claimed that words of classical origin should never be used in English. The distinctive contribution of Barnes to the controversy was to coin large numbers of compound words from native elements with the suggestion that they should replace familiar words borrowed from Latin or Greek. On the pattern of *lovelorn* he coined *reasonlorn* 'having lost one's reason' and *waylorn* 'having lost one's way'. The replacements that he suggested for grammatical terms show imagination but their meaning is not always self-evident. We can understand *thing-names* for 'nouns' without much trouble, but *breath-pennings* for 'consonants' is more difficult. *Pitches of suchness* for 'comparison of adjectives' has its own charm, but *time-words* for 'verbs' and *thought wording* for 'syntax' are misleading. Most of Barnes's coinages are now merely curiosities, quoted by those who wish to discredit his theories. They include such compounds as *folkdom* 'democracy', *folk-wain* 'omnibus' and *soaksome* 'bibulous'.

The word 'prescriptive' tends to be used as a term of abuse when applied to a grammarian, perhaps because a prescriptive reformer can never be wholly free from the risk of becoming proscriptive. To tell people that they ought to do something inevitably involves telling them that they ought to avoid doing the opposite. Yet the unpopularity of prescriptive grammarians is greater among philologists than with the general public. The popularity of the works of H. W. Fowler shows that there are many writers and speakers of English who are anxious to be told what to do and ready to follow the lead of anyone who tells them, provided that he writes confidently and gives the impression of being a reasonable man who does not require his readers to make any violent changes in their habits of speaking and writing.

Henry Watson Fowler (1858–1933) was a schoolmaster at Sedbergh for seventeen years. He resigned in 1899 and for the rest of his life devoted his considerable energies to lexicography, free-lance journalism and the production of two very popular books, *The King's English* (1906) and *A Dictionary of Modern English Usage* (1926). In the writing of the first of these and in the planning of the second he was helped by his younger brother Francis George, who died in 1917.

Otto Jespersen called Fowler an 'instinctive grammatical moralizer' and Fowler accepted the description. He held that a grammarian's function was to tell people 'not what they do and how they came to do it, but what he thinks they ought to do for the future'.[11] The time when people most readily consult Fowler is when they are trying to decide which of two words of similar form or meaning they should choose, as in the use of *intensive* or *intense*, on which the Prime Minister wrote in a minute to the Director of Military Intelligence in the Second World War: 'You should read Fowler's *Modern English Usage* on the use of the two words.'[12] On such matters Fowler's opinion carries weight, but he could be stubborn in maintaining his own opinion against opposition. For example, he refused to accept the useful distinction between *nem. con.* 'with no one dissenting' and *unanimously* 'with everyone agreeing'.[13] Fowler differed from other reformers, like William Barnes, in the wide range of subjects on which he expressed an opinion. When we remember Barnes we think at once of his antipathy to loan-words, but it is difficult to think of any one reform that we can associate with Fowler; we think rather of a multitude of minor points. A general feature of his approach is one that he shared with many earlier teachers of English, though it is one against which most philologists of today fight strenuously. It is a tendency to rely on the principles of Latin grammar in deciding what should be our approach to English, but on this, as on other matters, he was no extremist.

As a lexicographer Fowler realised the importance of a full treatment of common and everyday words as compared with a quest for those that are little-known. In carrying out this aim he was able to rely on the long entries for such words as *get* and *run*, which are a feature of the *OED*, and on which Fowler's *COD* was based.[14] The alphabetical arrangement, to which Fowler had become accustomed, was not well suited to the material presented in *Modern English Usage*, especially in view of his fondness for fanciful coinages as the title of articles. Sir Ernest Gowers says, in the Preface to the revised edition:

> it hardly deserves its title of 'dictionary', since much of it consists of short essays on various subjects, some with fancy titles that give no clue at all to their subject. What reporter, seeking guidance about the propriety of saying that the reception was held 'at the bride's aunt's', would think of looking for it in an article with the title 'Out of the Frying-Pan'? (pp. ii f.)

The Society for Pure English was founded in 1913 by a group of enthusiasts, chief of whom was the poet Robert Bridges. The founders made it clear that the use of the word 'pure' in the name of the Society was not intended to suggest that loan-words are impurities; they used the term 'Pure English' to mean 'Good English'. Their aims were excellent, but their expression of these aims sometimes seems rather smug. For example, Robert Bridges is apprehensive about the possible effect on the English language of its use by foreigners:

> There is furthermore this most obnoxious condition, namely, that wherever our countrymen are settled abroad there are alongside of them communities of other-speaking races, who, maintaining among themselves their native speech, learn yet enough of ours to mutilate it, and establishing among themselves all kinds of blundering corruptions through habitual intercourse infect therewith the neighbouring English (*The Society's Work*, SPE Tract No. 21, OUP, 1925, p. 5).

Although this sentence was written in 1925, it reflects attitudes that were already old-fashioned. There is real moral fervour in its denunciation of foreigners who make mistakes in the use of English, and there is possessiveness and a sort of linguistic imperialism in its attitude to English. It is no accident that it was published at the time of the Wembley British Empire Exhibition. The founders of the Society took themselves too seriously, and there is an air of cosy dilettantism about some of their activities. Robert Bridges was the only real enthusiast among the original committee of four. The others were Henry Bradley, an outstanding scholar, Logan Pearsall Smith, who from the first had misgivings, and Walter Raleigh, who was openly mocking. He wrote to Bridges: 'It's rather like proposing that everyone shall dress well and move gracefully'. The Society was nearly ruined at the start by the desire of Bridges and Raleigh to exercise a veto on membership. It was finally decided to accept as members all who paid an annual subscription of ten shillings, but the taint of cliquishness was never completely removed.

One of the aims of the Society was to prevent speech from growing out of touch with the great literature of the past. We see here the wish to retard the process of change which seems to afflict most linguistic reformers. We see too a wish to lessen the divergence between spoken and written language, but spoken and written English have their own traditions, and it is no good service to either to try to make people of today speak as the Elizabethans used to write.

The influence of the Society was strengthened by the inclusion among the members and authors of tracts of such eminent philologists as Henry Bradley and Sir William Craigie, and some of its tracts are important factual studies of various linguistic subjects that have a value quite independent of the aims of the Society's founders. Among the lesser aims put forward by these contributors were the introduction of useful dialect words into standard English and the encouragement of the coinage of new words to express new ideas. Between 1919 and 1948 the Society published sixty-six tracts, including studies of loan-words in English from Arabic (No. 38, 1933), Persian (No. 41, 1934), German (No. 42, 1934) and Dutch (No. 44, 1935). There were also studies of dialect, including G. N. Clark's *The Bull's Bellow* (No. 33, 1929) and Sir William A. Craigie's *Northern Words in Modern English* (No. 50, 1937), and many pamphlets on points of English usage by such scholars as the eminent Danish philologist Otto Jespersen. Although its achievement in reforming the language was probably small, the foundation of the Society was worth while, because it led to the publication of these studies which could with advantage be reprinted today.

Bridges was a man of many enthusiasms, and he rode one of his hobby-horses with vigour in the second of the tracts of the Society for Pure English: *On English Homophones* (1919). He reached a number of conclusions, which he expressed in characteristically forceful language. The chief of these, 'That homophones are a nuisance', is not likely to offend anybody, but he overstates his case. The number of occasions when homophones cause real ambiguity is very small, because the context usually makes it clear which of two homophones is intended. As Bridges pointed out, when the existence of homophones causes real difficulty in a language, because the two words are similar in function, one of the two words tends to become obsolete.

One of the best-known reformers during the present century was Sir Alan Herbert, perhaps better known as A. P. Herbert. There are resemblances between him and Swift. For both of them language was only one of many interests; both were persuasive and forceful controversialists, and both of them had common sense and intelligence without much linguistic knowledge, with the result that their writings on language contain much sound sense side by side with some folly.

A. P. Herbert realised the dangers of an excess of reforming zeal. He said 'When I have read a few columns in Mr H. W. Fowler's *Modern English Usage* I feel that I shall never dare to put pen to paper again'.[15] The chief object of his attack was the inflated polysyllabic language of public speeches and official announcements, but there were many other things that he disliked. He attacked clichés like 'acid test', 'bourgeois ideology' and 'a serious door', and pretentious pseudo-scientific phrases like 'a harmonious psycho-physiological equilibrium'.

Some of Herbert's views are exaggerated, such as his hatred of the useful prefix *re-*; it is using rather emotive language to describe *recondition* as 'a filthy verb'. When Herbert says that the verb *condition* 'stinks', it simply means that he does not like functional shift, the use of one part of speech for another, which has been a well-established feature of English for many centuries. This opinion is confirmed when we see in his index that *to contact* has the cross-reference 'See "Septic Verbs" '.

Herbert's antipathy to particular words was liable to depend on accidents of prejudice rather than on principles. Writing in 1935, he expresses his distaste for the verb *evacuate* in the sense 'send home from the firing-line' without realising that events would make the verb a vogue word in four years' time. He had a dislike, shared by many reformers, of any kind of semantic change. With a self-confidence that is only in part self-mockery he writes of the phrase 'the forces of reaction':

> Those who have been using it hitherto may plead ignorance, but after the publication of this work no Christian will have any excuse for speaking bitterly of 'the forces of reaction' again. The only true meaning of that is 'the forces which control the response of a body to the contact of another body' (p. 28).

So much for polysemy.

Herbert is intolerant of those who do not share his prejudices. He does not like the word *eventuality*: 'So we make an adjective out of 'event' – eventual: and some hog adds an 'ity' to the adjective and the solemn lexicographer welcomes the reptile into his book' (p. 31). He may be right or wrong in his dislike of *eventuality*, but he is certainly unjust to the lexicographer. A dictionary is not an anthology of words that appeal to the compiler, and his duty is to record what people say and write without omitting words on the grounds that he himself does not like them. To do his job does not involve solemnity, and the inclusion of a word does not necessarily involve welcome. Herbert knew that lexicographers took this view of their function, but he showed a debater's willingness to push it to one side when he took a different view. He suggested that words of which a lexicographer disapproves should be included with a black mark against them. Such a practice would be welcomed by many foreigners who, when using a dictionary, want to know something about a word's status, but comments of this kind should be made sparingly to avoid attaching too much importance to the opinion of the compiler and to allow for changes in acceptability that occur with the passage of time. A dictionary remains in use when usages that at first aroused bitter hostility have become generally accepted.

In general the influence of A. P. Herbert as a reformer was good. He hammered away unceasingly in his attacks on the pretentious use of words, and most readers are willing to forgive his excessive emphasis and his playful style, more appropriate to a nineteenth-century author of books for children. Even when he was wrong-headed, he served a useful purpose in making the readers of *Punch*, where his articles first appeared, think for themselves about the use of words in the attempt to confute him.

A reformer who, without being a philologist, tried to get to grips with the English language was Stuart Chase, an American accountant and economist, whose *The Tyranny of Words* (Methuen, 1938) is a popularisation of what has come to be known as general semantics. His favourite theme is the over-use of abstract words without sufficient care to understand exactly what they mean. One of his many examples is a passage from Bergson:

> Intuition may be described as turning past and present into fact directly known by transferring it from mere matter into a creative process of duration.

This quotation is followed by a 'semantic translation':

> Intuition may be described as turning blab and blab into blab directly known by blabbing it from mere matter into a blab blab of blab (p. 152).

This is too easy. To say what is the exact meaning of an abstract term is both important and difficult, but to say that words like 'past' and 'present' are entirely meaningless is defeatism. Chase's approach is too much like that of the writer of a testimonial who uses 'I don't know' as an implied condemnation. Nevertheless Chase's influence has been salutary in that he calls attention to a common fault in writing that is on the increase: the use of long abstract words as a substitute for thought or as a screen for hostile propaganda.

The correspondence columns of newspapers provide evidence that their readers take a lively interest in the English language and its reform. Some of the letters deal with well-worn subjects such as functional shift or the borrowing of words from American English; others discuss points of detail. One subject of frequent hostile comment is the use of hybrid words, words made up of elements borrowed from different languages. Such words are very common in English and there is no reason at all why they should not continue to flourish. An example often quoted is *macadamised*, with elements from four different languages. But even so judicious an author as Theodore H. Savory, author of *The Language of Science* (Andre Deutsch, 1953) takes antipathy for granted. After quoting words like *haemoglobin* and *micronucleus*, of which the first element is Greek and the second Latin, he says:

> These words are called hybrids, and their appearance, their use and their persistence cannot be described as anything but lamentable. Students of literary English are agreed in regarding these words as undesirable (p. 54).

Students of literary English are not so agreed.

Other reformers have allowed a knowledge of etymology to go to their heads. If *cinema* is ultimately derived from a Greek word beginning with kappa, they will say that the *c* should be pronounced [k], forgetting that the immediate source is often more important than the ultimate etymology. If the word is immediately borrowed from French, [s] is a more reasonable pronunciation. Whatever the etymology, there is a lot to be said for a pronunciation in accordance with the usual conventions of English spelling without introducing anomalies.

Some changes are quickly accepted and cease to be noticed by the majority of readers while others pass out of use.

Among the innovations that are currently noticeable may be mentioned such prolixities as *at this moment in time* for 'now' and the use of *situation* preceded by an abstract noun to replace an adjective. A pregnant women is described as being in a pregnancy situation, and the owners of a theatre, hoping that it will stop losing money, say that it will soon be in a profitability situation. Some of the most common words in the language, whose chief function is to denote the relation between other words, are under attack. No one can feel that he is showing much originality by using the word *and*, so many people are now replacing it by *plus*, probably under the influence of commercial language, when an advertiser introduces the last of the ingredients of a special offer by a triumphant *plus*, followed by a pause to heighten expectancy. The currently popular use of *into* to indicate an interest, as when we say that someone is into computers, is probably borrowed from the language of the stock exchange. Other current trends affecting common words are the use of *following* to mean 'after' and *in excess of* to mean 'more than'. The latter vogue usage may convey an idea not intended by the speaker, since 'excess' has pejorative associations with something wasteful and ridiculous that are not present in the colourless 'more than'. Two vogue-words that are enjoying great popularity at present are *massive* and *sad*. Anyone asking for the spending of a large sum of money is likely to describe it as massive aid and, when reporting that somebody does not agree with him, he is liable to say that such disagreement makes him sad.

In recent years there has been a change in the attitude of those whose linguistic habits provoke censure. Speakers whose use of words would in the past have been unhesitatingly condemned as slipshod have learnt that the best form of defence is attack, and they have begun to defend their speech habits on the grounds that the supposed rules are broken more often than they are observed and are therefore no longer valid. There is a grain of truth in this appeal to usage but it should not be accepted without examination. Usage is one of the factors to be taken into account, but it should not be allowed to override all other considerations. In discussing questions of usage we are concerned not merely with the size of the majority but with its quality. Opinions will differ about the importance of the size of the majority. One view was expressed by Hamlet in his advice to the Players not to o'erstep the modesty of nature:

> Now this overdone, or come tardy off, though it make the unskilful laugh, cannot but make the judicious grieve; the censure of the which one must in your allowance o'erweigh a whole theatre of others (*Hamlet*, III, 2.29–33).

It is more important to ask whether the distinction is a useful one. Many people use *infer* in the sense 'imply', but the distinction between *infer* and *imply* is worth preserving and can be briefly stated: the hearer infers what the speaker implies. The accident that the two words *flout* and *flaunt* have three consonants in common leads to confusion between the two words, though their meanings are wide apart: *to flaunt* is to make a parade of something while *to flout* is to show a contemptuous disregard for it. Some words are confused because of the addition of a suffix and because those who use them feel that a long word must be better than a short one. Thus we find *intensive* used for *intense*, *definitive* for *definite*, and *alternative* for *alternate*.

The heat engendered by discussions on usage is a matter for surprise. A writer who maintained that there is a distinction in meaning between *uninterested* 'not interested' and *disinterested* 'impartial' provoked a hostile comment from a critic who claimed that most people make no distinction. One wonders how the critic knows what most people think. Opinions on usage are not generally based on carefully chosen samples of speakers; they are based on such examples of the speech of the critic's acquaintances or the books that he has read as he happens to have noticed. It may seem at first to be a matter for congratulation that the participants in such discussions are so interested in linguistic matters as to express themselves strongly, but it is to be feared that other motives are present, as in the heated discussions that take place on which words are U and which are non-U. The indignation shown by those who attack what they regard as substandard usage may spring from the intolerance that makes many people act on the assumption that everything that is not compulsory should be forbidden, and the indignation of the defenders may arise from the anger that we all feel when our behaviour is criticised. A plea for tolerance in linguistic matters does not rest upon the belief that they are unimportant but on a conviction that there is something to be said on both sides and that there is room for variety. In matters of language, as in other matters, there is a lot to be said for saying simply that their nonsense doesn't suit our nonsense and continuing to make the distinctions that we think important in the belief that, if we are right, those readers whose opinion we value will have reached the same conclusion and that careful writers will go on making those distinctions even if they are outvoted.

Distinctions of the kind that have here been illustrated are trivial in comparison with the large number of words and phrases that go to make up the English language. Those who ignore them have failed to make the best use of the language, but so do we all sometimes. The misuse of language that calls for really strong condemnation is that which deliberately uses language to confuse moral issues. It was the use of such language by Boswell in speaking of the divorce of Lady Diana Beauclerk which occasioned Dr Johnson's robust rebuke, recorded by Boswell:

> Seduced, perhaps, by the charms of the lady in question, I thus attempted to palliate what I was sensible could not be justified; for, when I had finished my harangue, my venerable friend gave me a proper check: 'My dear Sir, never accustom your mind to mingle virtue and vice. The woman's a whore, and there's an end on't'.[16]

Those who are fond of making the worse appear the better reason sometimes quote literary parallels which are based on a complete misinterpretation of character. The hero of James Thurber's *The Secret Life of Walter Mitty* is a likeable and thoroughly disinterested character who takes refuge from an unhappy life by indulging in day-dreams. With monotonous frequency he is used by barristers defending a liar and confidence trickster who has deceived other people but not himself but who is presented as 'a Walter Mitty type of character'.

Sometimes a group of reformers will concentrate upon a

single word and give it what seems to be an undue amount of attention. Most of us, uncertain what all the fuss is about, but anxious to avoid giving offence, usually acquiesce in quite arbitrary conventions that are imposed on us and try to avoid applying the adjective *Scotch* to a human being or speaking of a *serviette* instead of a *napkin*. Only occasionally does common sense revolt, as at the use of *chairperson* to make it clear that the word may refer to a woman. The primary meaning of *man* is 'human being' as distinct from other animals, and when we say that man is born unto trouble as the sparks fly upward or that he is a political animal, only a fool would assume that we mean that a woman isn't. The restriction of *man* to mean 'adult human male' is one of several later developments in the meaning of the word, and it does not need a philologist to tell us that a word can have several different meanings.

One general conclusion can be drawn from the efforts of the reformers, a conclusion which will cause disquiet to some while it brings consolation to others. This is that the language is capable of putting up very strong resistance to the efforts of those who try to change it or to prevent it from changing. Those who find the language unsatisfactory are right in trying to improve it, but their efforts will have very little effect on the language as a whole.

Notes and References

Place of publication is London unless otherwise stated.

CHAPTER 1

1. Edmund Crispin, *Love Lies Bleeding* (Gollancz, 1948).
2. 'In praise of Roget' in *Words* (BBC, 1975) p. 113.
3. Christopher Hassall, *Rupert Brooke: A Biography* (Faber, 1964) p. 90.
4. See Logan Pearsall Smith, 'Dialectal and Popular Words' in *A Few Practical Suggestions* (SPE Tract No. 3, OUP, 1920) p. 9.
5. Marghanita Laski, 'Deep deep feeling' in *Words* (BBC, 1975) p. 29.
6. Ben Jonson, *Poetaster* (1602) V.3. 465–530.
7. Logan Pearsall Smith, *Words and Idioms* (Constable, 1925) p. 138.
8. Logan Pearsall Smith, *Words and Idioms* (Constable, 1925) p. 258. In the treatment of idioms I have been greatly helped by the essay on 'English Idioms' in this book.
9. Kenneth Hudson, *The Dictionary of Diseased English* (Macmillan, 1977) p. 1.

CHAPTER 2

1. See Otto Jespersen, *Growth and Structure of the English Language* (Blackwell, eighth edition, 1935) ch. v; Mary S. Serjeantson, *A History of Foreign Words in English* (Kegan Paul, 1935) ch. V; and J. A. Sheard, *The Words We Use* (Andre Deutsch, 1954) ch. vi.
2. Mary S. Serjeantson, *A History of Foreign Words in English*, pp. 161 f.
3. Leo Rosten, *The Joys of Yiddish* (Penguin, 1971) pp. xiii f.

CHAPTER 3

1. Anthony Powell, in a review in the *Daily Telegraph*, 15 September 1977.

CHAPTER 4

1. E. M. Wright, *Rustic Speech and Folk-lore* (OUP, 1914) p. 6.
2. See map on p. 37 of G. L. Brook, *English Dialects* (Andre Deutsch, 1963).

3. Peter Wright, *The Language of British Industry* (Macmillan, 1974) pp. 140 f.
4. See Sir William A. Craigie, *Northern Words in Modern English*, (SPE Tract No. 50, OUP, 1937).
5. Logan Pearsall Smith, *Words and Idioms* (Constable, 1925) p. 161.
6. *Daily Telegraph*, 12 July 1976.
7. Richard Hoggart, in the Foreword to Kenneth Hudson's *The Dictionary of Diseased English* (Macmillan, 1977) p. vii.
8. Kenneth Hudson, *The Dictionary of Diseased English* (Macmillan, 1977) p. xxvii.
9. Henry Bradley, *The Making of English*, revised by Simeon Potter (Macmillan, 1968) pp. 72 f.
10. T. H. Savory, *The Language of Science* (Andre Deutsch, 1953) pp. 52 f.
11. Edmund Sandars, *An Insect Book for the Pocket* (OUP, 1946) p. 8.
12. E. G. Boulenger, *World Natural History* (Batsford, 1937) p. 67.
13. Elizabeth Mary Wright, *Rustic Speech and Folk-Lore* (OUP, 1914) p. 7.
14. Philip Howard, *New Words for Old* (Hamish Hamilton, 1977) p. 60.
15. Mario Pei, *The Story of English* (Allen and Unwin, 1953) p. 224.
16. Sean Jennett, *The Making of Books* (Faber, 1951) p. 48.
17. David Crystal and Derek Davy, *Investigating English Style* (Longman, 1969) p. 208.
18. P. G. Osborn, *A Concise Law Dictionary* (Sweet and Maxwell, fifth edition, 1964) p. 119. I am indebted to Mr Stuart Harling Ll B for this reference.
19. Lord Strang, *The Diplomatic Career* (Andre Deutsch, 1962) p. 64. Quoted from Kenneth Hudson, *The Language of Modern Politics* (Macmillan, 1978) pp. 78–9.
20. Philip Howard, *Weasel Words* (Hamish Hamilton, 1978) p. 13.

CHAPTER 5

1. C. S. Lewis, *Studies in Words* (CUP, 1960) p. 141.
2. J. B. Greenough and G. L. Kittredge, *Words and their Ways in English Speech* (Macmillan, 1902) p. 291.
3. George H. McKnight, *Modern English in the Making* (New York: Appleton-Century-Crofts, 1928) p. 412.
4. Philip Howard, *New Words for Old* (Hamish Hamilton, 1977) p. 86.

CHAPTER 6

1. G. W. Turner, *Stylistics* (Penguin, 1973) p. 112.
2. For a fuller treatment of prefixes and suffixes see Brian Foster, *The Changing English Language* (Macmillan, 1968) pp. 170–92, and Barbara M. H. Strang, *A History of English* (Methuen, 1970) pp. 88–90, 188–92, 337.
3. Logan Pearsall Smith, *Words and Idioms* (Constable, 1925) p. 24.
4. J. A. Sheard, *The Words We Use* (Andre Deutsch, 1954) p. 75.

CHAPTER 7

1. Robert Graves and Alan Hodge, *The Reader over your Shoulder* (Cape, 1943), p. 209.
2. Geoffrey Leech, *A Linguistic Guide to English Poetry* (Longman, 1969) p. 77.
3. J. I. M. Stewart, *The Gaudy* (Gollancz, 1974) ch. 1.
4. Winifred Nowottny, *The Language Poets Use* (Athlone Press, 1962) p. 67.
5. Gibbon, *The Decline and Fall of the Roman Empire*, edited by J. B. Bury (Methuen, 1897) vol. I, p. 337.
6. George Mikes, *How to be an Alien* (Andre Deutsch, 1946) pp. 39–40.
7. Philip Howard, *Weasel Words* (Hamish Hamilton, 1978) p. 98.
8. Geoffrey Leech, *A Linguistic Guide to English Poetry*, p. 171.
9. Max Beerbohm, in *More* (1899).
10. A. C. Baugh, *A History of the English Language* (Routledge, 1951) p. 284.
11. Ben Jonson, *Discoveries* (1641) – edited by G. B. Harrison (Bodley Head Quartos, 1923) p. 70.
12. Winifred Nowottny, *The Language Poets Use*, p. 146.
13. George H. McKnight, *English Words and their Background* (New York: Appleton, 1923) p. 396.
14. Stella Brook, *The Language of the Book of Common Prayer* (Andre Deutsch, 1965) p. 133.
15. Sir Ernest Gowers, *The Complete Plain Words* (Penguin, 1962) p. 20.
16. See Albert C. Baugh, *A History of the English Language* (Routledge and Kegan Paul, 1951) p. 283.
17. J. A. Sheard, *The Words We Use* (Andre Deutsch, 1954) p. 296.

CHAPTER 8

1. David Crystal and Derek Davy, *Investigating English Style* (Longman, 1969) p. 148.
2. Stella Brook, *The Language of the Book of Common Prayer* (Andre Deutsch, 1965) p. 130.
3. A. C. Partridge, *English Biblical Translation* (Andre Deutsch, 1973) p. 5.
4. Bernard Groom, *A Short History of English Words* (Macmillan, 1934) p. 149.
5. Sir Frederic Kenyon, *The Reading of the Bible* (John Murray, 1944) pp. 69 f.
6. See Bernard Groom, *A Short History of English Words*, pp. 145–8, and J. A. Sheard, *The Words We Use* (Andre Deutsch, 1954) pp. 292f.
7. For information about the vocabulary of the Authorised Version, especially in recording the number of occurrences of particular words, I am indebted to Ronald Bridges and Luther A. Weigle, *The Bible Word Book* (New York: Nelson, 1960).
8. Don Cupitt, 'Metaphorically speaking', in *Words* (BBC, 1975) p. 102.
9. C. S. Lewis, *The Literary Impact of the Authorised Version* (Athlone Press, 1950) p. 16.
10. Richard Graves, *The Spiritual Quixote* (1773) bk I, ch. 9.

CHAPTER 9

1. See G. L. Brook, *The Language of Dickens* (Andre Deutsch, 1970) pp. 176–9.
2. By Susie I. Tucker in *English Examined: Two centuries of comment on the mother-tongue* (CUP, 1961).
3. R. F. Jones, *The Triumph of the English Language* (Stanford University Press, 1953) pp. 199 f.
4. The examples are quoted from R. F. Jones, *The Triumph of the English Language*, pp. 135 f.
5. *Essays of John Dryden*, selected and edited by W. P. Ker (OUP, 1900) pp. 234 f.
6. Quoted from Susie I. Tucker, *English Examined*, p. 92.
7. Robert Heron, *Letters of Literature* (1785) pp. 240–9. Quoted from W. S. Lewis (ed.), *The Yale Edition of Horace Walpole's Correspondence*, vol. 16, p. 264.
8. Daniel Defoe, 'Of Academies', *An Essay upon Several Projects* (1702), pp. 228 ff, quoted from Susie I. Tucker, *English Examined*, pp. 58–60.
9. Jonathan Swift, *A Proposal for Correcting, Improving and Ascertaining the English Tongue* (1712), in Herbert Davis with Louis Landa (eds), *The Prose Writings of Jonathan Swift* (Blackwell, 1957) p. 14.
10. Reprinted in Giles Dugdale, *William Barnes of Dorset* (Cassell, 1953) appx 3.
11. H. W. Fowler, 'Professor Jespersen and "the Instinctive Grammatical Moralizer" ' in SPE Tract No. 26 (OUP, 1927) p. 194.
12. Sir Ernest Gowers, Preface to the revised edition of *A Dictionary of Modern English Usage* (OUP, 1965) p. iii.
13. R. W. Burchfield, *The Fowlers: their Achievements in Lexicography and Grammar* (English Association Presidential Address, 1979) p. 17.
14. R. W. Burchfield, *The Fowlers*, p. 13.
15. A. P. Herbert, *What a Word!* (Methuen, 1935) p. 2.
16. Boswell's *Life of Johnson*, edited by George Birkbeck Hill, revised by L. F. Powell (OUP, 1934) vol. II, p. 247.

Bibliography

Place of publication is London unless otherwise stated.

Bacquet, Paul, *L'Étymologie anglaise* (Paris: Presses Universitaires de France, 1976).

Bacquet, Paul, *Le Vocabulaire anglais* (Paris: Presses Universitaires de France, 1974).

Barber, Charles, *Linguistic Change in Present-day English* (Edinburgh: Oliver and Boyd, 1964).

Barfield, Owen, *History in English Words* (Methuen, 1926).

Baugh, Albert C., *A History of the English Language* (Routledge and Kegan Paul, 1951; 2nd edn, 1959).

Bradley, Henry, *The Making of English* (1904). Revised by Simeon Potter (Macmillan, 1968).

Bridges, Ronald, and Weigle, Luther A., *The Bible Word Book: Concerning Obsolete or Archaic Words in the King James Version of the Bible* (New York: Thomas Nelson, 1960).

Brook, G. L., *English Dialects* (Andre Deutsch, 1963; 3rd edn, 1978).

Brook, G. L., *Varieties of English* (Macmillan, 1973; 2nd edn, 1979).

Brook, Stella, *The Language of the Book of Common Prayer* (Andre Deutsch, 1965).

Bryant, Margaret M., *Modern English and its Heritage* (New York: Macmillan, 1950).

Burchfield, R. W. (ed.), *A Supplement to the Oxford English Dictionary*, vol. I A–G, vol. II H–N, vol. III O–Scz (OUP, 1972–82)

Chase, Stuart, *The Tyranny of Words* (Methuen, 1938).

The Concise Oxford Dictionary of Current English, edited by H. W. Fowler and F. G. Fowler (OUP, 1911; 6th edn edited by J. B. Sykes, 1976).

Crystal, David, and Davy, Derek, *Investigating English Style* (Longman, 1969).

Dryden, John, *Essays*, selected and edited by W. P. Ker, 2 vols (OUP, 1900).

Eichner, Hans (ed.), *'Romantic' and its Cognates: the European History of a Word* (Manchester University Press, 1972).

Foster, Brian, *The Changing English Language* (Macmillan, 1968).

Fowler, H. W., *A Dictionary of Modern English Usage* (OUP, 1926; 2nd edn revised by Sir Ernest Gowers, 1965).

Fowler, Roger (ed.), *Essays on Style and Language: Linguistic and Critical Approaches to Literary Style* (Routledge and Kegan Paul, 1966).

Fowler, Roger, *The Languages of Literature: Some Linguistic Contributions to Criticism* (Routledge and Kegan Paul, 1971).

Gordon, Ian A., *The Movement of English Prose* (Longman, 1966).

Gowers, Sir Ernest, *The Complete Plain Words* (Penguin, 1962). This book incorporates *Plain Words* (1948) and *The ABC of Plain Words* (1951).

Graves, Robert, and Hodge, Alan, *The Reader Over Your Shoulder: a Handbook for Writers of English Prose* (Cape, 1943).

Greenough, James Bradstreet, and Kittredge, George Lyman, *Words and their Ways in English Speech* (Macmillan, 1902).

Groom, Bernard, *A Short History of English Words* (Macmillan, 1934).

Herbert, A. P., *What a Word!* (Methuen, 1935).

Horwill, H. W., *A Dictionary of Modern American Usage* (OUP, 1935).

Howard, Philip, *New Words for Old* (Hamish Hamilton, 1977).

Howard, Philip, *Weasel Words* (Hamish Hamilton, 1978).

Hudson, Kenneth, *The Dictionary of Diseased English* (Macmillan, 1977).

Hudson, Kenneth, *The Jargon of the Professions* (Macmillan, 1978).

Hudson, Kenneth, *The Language of Modern Politics* (Macmillan, 1978).

Jespersen, Otto, *Growth and Structure of the English Language* (1909; 8th edn, Oxford: Blackwell, 1935).

Jones, Richard Foster, *The Triumph of the English Language: a Survey of Opinions Concerning the Vernacular from the*

Introduction of Printing to the Restoration (Stanford, California: Stanford University Press, 1953).

Kenyon, Sir Frederic, *The Reading of the Bible as History, as Literature and as Religion* (Murray, 1944).

Leech, Geoffrey N., *English in Advertising: a Linguistic study of Advertising in Great Britain* (Longman, 1966).

Leech, Geoffrey N., *A Linguistic Guide to English Poetry* (Longman, 1969).

Lewis, C. S., *The Literary Impact of the Authorised Version* (Athlone Press, 1950).

Lewis, C. S. *Studies in Words* (CUP, 1960).

McKnight, George H., *English Words and their Background* (New York: Appleton-Century, 1923).

McKnight, George H., with the assistance of Bert Emsley, *Modern English in the Making* (New York: Appleton-Century-Crofts, 1928).

Mencken, H. L., *The American Language* (Kegan Paul, 4th edn, 1936; supplements I and II, New York: Knopf, 1948).

Mulcaster, Richard, *The First Part of the Elementary 1952* (Menston: Scolar Press, 1970 – a Scolar Press facsimile).

The New English Dictionary on Historical Principles, edited by J. A. H. Murray, Henry Bradley, W. A. Craigie and C. T. Onions (1884–1928). Re-issued as *The Oxford English Dictionary* in twelve volumes and a supplement (OUP, 1933).

Nowottny, Winifred, *The Language Poets Use* (Athlone Press, 1962).

Onions, C. T. (ed.), *The Oxford Dictionary of English Etymology* (OUP, 1966).

Onions, C. T., *A Shakespeare Glossary* (OUP, 1911; 2nd edn., 1919).

Partridge, A. C. *English Biblical Translation* (Andre Deutsch, 1973).

Partridge, Eric, *A Dictionary of Slang and Unconventional English* (Routledge and Kegan Paul, 1937; 6th edn, 2 vols, 1967).

Partridge, Eric, *Name into Word: Proper Names that have Become Common Property* (Secker and Warburg, 1949).

Partridge, Eric, *Slang To-day and Yesterday* (Routledge, 2nd edn., 1935).

Pei, Mario, *The Story of English* (Allen and Unwin, 1953).

Praz, Mario, 'The Italian Element in English' in *Essays and Studies by Members of the English Association*, vol. XV (OUP, 1929) pp. 20–66.

Quirk, Randolph, *The Use of English*, with supplements by A. C. Gimson and Jeremy Warburg (Longman, 1962; 2nd edn., 1968).

Robertson, Stuart, *The Development of Modern English* (New York: Prentice-Hall, 1934). A new edition, revised by F. G. Cassidy, was published in 1954.

Rosten, Leo, *The Joys of Yiddish* (Penguin, 1971; first published in the USA in 1968).

Serjeantson, Mary, *A History of Foreign Words in English* (Kegan Paul, 1935).

Sheard, J. A., *The Words We Use* (Andre Deutsch, 1954).

Smith, Logan Pearsall, *Words and Idioms: Studies in the English Language* (Constable, 1925).

Stern, Gustaf, *Meaning and Change of Meaning* (Gothenburg, 1931; reprinted, Bloomington: Indiana University Press, 1931).

Strang, Barbara M. H., *A History of English* (Methuen, 1970).

Tucker, Susie I. (ed.), *English Examined: Two Centuries of Comment on the Mother-tongue* (CUP, 1961).

Turner, G. W., *Stylistics* (Penguin, 1973).

Ullmann, Stephen, *Semantics: an Introduction to the Science of Meaning* (Oxford: Blackwell, 1962).

Ullmann, Stephen, *Words and their Use* (Muller, 1951).

Wakelin, Martyn F., *English Dialects: an Introduction* (Athlone Press, 1972).

Wakelin, Martyn F. (ed.), *Patterns in the Folk Speech of the British Isles* (Athlone Press, 1972).

Words: Reflections on the Use of Language (BBC, 1975). Brief essays by fourteen authors, with Preface by Ian McIntyre.

Wright, Peter, *The Language of British Industry* (Macmillan, 1974).

Zandvoort, R. W., and assistants, *Wartime English: Materials for a Linguistic History of World War II* (Groningen: Wolters, 1957).

Index

Words, but not phrases, quoted as examples are included in *italics*. No references are given to the Bibliography.

The manufacturer's authorised representative in the EU is Springer Nature Customer Service Centre GmbH, Europaplatz 3, 69115 Heidelberg, Germany. If you have any concerns regarding our products, please contact ProductSafety@springernature.com

Printed and bound by CPI Group (UK) Ltd, Croydon, CR0 4YY

23/03/2026

02076673-0011